ENEMIES

ENEMIES

Maxim Gorky

Translated by
Kitty Hunter-Blair and Jeremy Brooks

With an Introduction by Edward Braun
and a Preface by Jeremy Brooks

THE VIKING PRESS · NEW YORK
A Richard Seaver Book

A Richard Seaver Book / The Viking Press

Published in 1972 in a hardbound and paperbound edition by
The Viking Press, Inc., 625 Madison Avenue, New York, N.Y. 10022

SBN 670-29492-6 (hardbound)
670-00373-5 (paperbound)
Library of Congress catalog card number: 72-80999
Printed in U.S.A.

Second printing June 1974

Maxim Gorky

1868   Born, Alexey Maximovich Peshkov, in Nizhni Novgorod, 225 miles east of Moscow. Mother from a family of dyers, father an upholsterer, later a wharf manager.

1872   Father dies. Mother abandons Alexey, who is brought up by Grandmother.

1878   Mother dies. Grandfather sends the boy away to earn his own living.

1878–1884   Nomadic labourer – boot boy, errand boy, bird catcher, dishwasher on a Volga paddleboat, assistant in an icon shop. Self-education begins.

1884   Arrives in Kazan, hoping to enter University, but fails to get a place. Works as stevedore, meets students, intellectuals, revolutionaries. Works in a bakery. Toys with Populism, Tolstoyism, dreams of setting up a Tolstoyan commune. Is invited to become a police spy. Studies the violin, tries to fall in love, fails at both. News of Grandmother's death reaches him.

1887   Tries to commit suicide, succeeds in damaging left lung.

1888   Working in an up-Volga fishery, then as railway nightwatchman. Arrives in Moscow, horrified by it, heads back towards Nizhni Novgorod. Calls at Yasnaya Polyana, is given rolls and coffee in the kitchen by Tolstoy's wife. Is beaten nearly to death by Cossacks for trying to intercede for an adulteress who is being dragged naked behind a horse. Is hospitalized.

1889   Attempts to enrol as an army engineer, rejected as politically unreliable. Shows his writings to elderly Populist writer Korolenko, whose gentle criticisms cause him to tear up his MSS and resolve never to write again. Succeeds in falling in love with a married woman, Olga.

1892   Runs away from Olga to Tiflis, and a job on a local newspaper, which publishes his first story, *Makar Chudra*.

1892–1894   Lives with Olga in a Nizhni bathhouse, causing great scandal. Olga oppressed by his romanticism, he by her flirtations with other men.

1894   Leaves Olga to work on a newspaper in Samara.

1895   Korolenko publishes a new story, *Chelkash*, in his magazine over the name 'Maxim Gorky' – chosen by Gorky on the spur of the moment. 'Gorky' means 'The Bitter'.

1896   Marries a gymnasia student, a proof-reader on the Samara *Gazette*, and a Populist radical. She bears him a son, Maxim. Toys with Marxism. Contracts tuberculosis, recuperates in the Crimea, paid for by a literary fund.

1897   Returns to Nizhni, is arrested for giving 'seditious readings' and sent to prison in Tiflis. A Marxist journalist pulls strings, and he is allowed to go back to Nizhni and live 'under surveillance' – remains under it until the Revolution. Is ill again, can't work; but an advance on the publication of his collected stories keeps him and his family alive.

1898   *Stories and Sketches* published, an immediate success, over 100,000 copies sold – unique in Russia's book publishing history. Gorky instantly famous. Corresponds warmly with Chekhov.

1899   Meets Chekhov at Yalta.

1900   Introduced by Chekhov to Tolstoy. Is offended by Tolstoy's obscene language. Tolstoy finds Gorky 'better than his writings'. Publishes his first novel, *Foma Gordeyev*, closely followed by a second, *The Three of Them*. Joins a group of writers and artists in Moscow called 'The Knowledge Group'. Is embarrassed by the adulation of Moscow crowds. Nicknamed 'The Falcon'. Befriended by artists from Moscow Art Theatre, is encouraged to write a play. Starts work on *The Lower Depths*, but finishes an offshoot of this, *The Philistines*, first.

1902   Exiled by the police to Arzamas, finishes *The Lower Depths*. *The Philistines* refused a licence, but, with cuts, is allowed to be performed for subscribers of the Art Theatre only, with uniformed police as ticket collectors. In the provinces the play provokes riots. Gorky's nickname changed to 'Stormy Petrel'.

Dec. 1902   *The Lower Depths* staged in Moscow – 'thrilled and stirred' the middle-class audience, then sweeps the world's capitals. 75,000 copies of the play sold in a year. Gorky's American publisher states that his fame now surpasses Tolstoy's. Gorky turns over much of his private funds to the Social Democratic Party, after meeting some of Lenin's followers in Moscow.

1903   'Knowledge' becomes a co-operative publishing house.

1904   Writes *Summer Folk*, a play heavily influenced by Chekhov.

1905   Is involved with the priest, Gapon, in organizing the workers' march on the Winter Palace. Joins delegation of intellectuals to the Minister of the Interior to plead for no violence. After the slaughter of 'Bloody Sunday' Gapon flees to Gorky's apartment, is disguised, leaves Russia. Two days later Gorky is arrested, imprisoned in the Peter and Paul Fortress, where he writes *Children of the Sun*, one of his best plays. Pressure from the West, and bail money from a power-mad industrialist who thought he could 'buy the revolution', gets him out of prison.

Dec. 1905   Involved in organizing support for the workers' barricades in Moscow during the last gasp of the '1905 Revolution'. Pursued by police, he flees to Finland, thence to Berlin.

1906   What was to have been a triumphal fund-raising tour of the United States aborted by press disclosures that the 'Mme Gorky' he lives with is not his wife, but a Moscow Art Theatre actress. Publicly spurned by the famous, Gorky goes into retreat, writes *The Mother*, a novel welcomed by Lenin as 'an instrument of revolution'. Completes *Enemies*. Settles on Capri.

1907   *Enemies* staged by Max Reinhardt at the Kleines Theater, Berlin. Attends Fifth Congress of Social

Democratic Party in Brussels and London. Is not (and never became) a member of the Party. Meets Lenin and Trotsky. Returns to Capri, writes two novels.

1908   Writes *The Confession*, reveals his religious attitude towards revolution. With Bogdanov and Lunacharsky sets up a school for revolutionary Russian workers. Leading Mensheviks, suspecting Gorky's attachment to Lenin, refuse to come and lecture; Lenin, angry about *The Confession*, and preparing to expel Bogdanov from the Party, also refuses to come.

1909   Constant correspondence from Lenin, who fosters factionalism at the school, succeeds in driving Bogdanov out.

1910   Lenin visits Capri. Gorky writes two more novels.

1911–1912   Remains in retreat on Capri, writing many stories, including the powerful *Twenty-six and One*. His play, *Vassa Zheleznova* (*The Mother*) awarded Griboyedov Prize in Moscow.

1913   Writes *Childhood*, published serially in a newspaper. On the 300th anniversary of the Romanov dynasty an amnesty for political exiles is granted. Gorky returns cautiously to Russia. Breaks with Lenin, who keeps writing friendly letters but gets no replies.

1914–1917   Writes several autobiographical works. Opposes Russia's participation in the Great War. Founds two magazines and a newspaper, *New Life*, which becomes the most widely read newssheet among the intelligentsia. Attacked as a bolshevik and pro-German by the Right, and as a proponent of 'false unification' by the Leninist Left. After the February 1917 Revolution, opposes Lenin's plans for a further bolshevik uprising.

1918–1921   *New Life* the only independent journal in Russia. Gorky continues to oppose the new regime, attacks Lenin as 'the mad chemist'. *New Life* finally forced to close down. Gorky allows himself to be reconciled with Lenin. But Zinoviev, an old enemy, is after Gorky's blood; Lenin pleads with him to leave Russia 'to recuperate'.

1922–1924   Travels about Europe. Writes a film scenario, *Stepan Razin*, which is a clear condemnation of Lenin's attitudes, and his *Reminiscences* of Tolstoy, Chekhov and Andreyev.

1924–1930   Settles in Sorrento. Visited by his legal wife and their son. Writes *My Universities, Fragments*. Is mercilessly sponged on by other exiles.

1928   Nizhni Novgorod renamed Gorky – part of Stalin's campaign to persuade Gorky to return to Russia. Gorky visits Russia and is given red carpet treatment.

1929   Another visit to Russia. Gorky shown a huge collective farm and a 'humane' concentration camp – both specially prepared for his benefit.

1931–1932   Completes three last plays, *Somov and Others, Yegor Bulchychov and Others* and *Dostigayev and Others*. Returns to Russia for good. Is given funds to start publishing houses, magazines, writers' collectives.

1933   Gorky now a 'superintendent of writers'.

1934   Head of Writers' Union. His son, Maxim, dies – almost certainly liquidated.

1935   Rewrites his early plays, *The Zikovs* and *The Last Ones*, so that both plays reflect his knowledge that the Revolution had somehow gone wrong. He applies for a passport, is refused.

1936   Second application for a passport refused. Gorky knows that time has run out for him. Stalin is preparing the ground for the Great Purges, can't afford to have someone of Gorky's international weight around. On 19th June Gorky dies, in circumstances never clarified. By the end of the year, all who attended his death are also dead.

Introduction

Gorky's association with the theatre dates from 1900 when Chekhov introduced him to the Moscow Art Theatre company who had brought their productions of *The Seagull* and *Uncle Vanya* to the Crimea for the benefit of the convalescent author. Encouraged by Stanislavsky and Nemirovich-Danchenko, Gorky was soon at work on scenes depicting 'a lodging house, foul air, trestle beds, a long dreary winter' and eventually called *The Lower Depths*. Between 1902 and 1915 he completed some fourteen plays, but until the 'thirties his theatrical reputation rested almost entirely on this one work. Presented by the Art Theatre in December 1902, it immediately overshadowed their production of *Philistines* which had been staged nine months earlier. In this first play Gorky contrasts the pettiness of the lower-middle class in Russia with the vigour and optimism of the 'new man' of proletarian stock. It was treated with a degree of suspicion remarkable even for the Tsarist censor and performed amidst police precautions more appropriate to a mass rally than to the select audience of regular theatre subscribers. Almost inevitably it proved a mild anti-climax both in Petersburg on tour and back in Moscow, partly because of the mutilation suffered by the text, partly because of its own looseness of form, but equally because of the company's inability to grasp its full social implications. On Chekhov at least its significance was not lost; referring to the play in 1903, he wrote:

> Gorky is the first in Russia and in the world at large to have expressed contempt and loathing for the petty bourgeoisie and he has done it at the precise moment when society is ready for protest.*

Like Chekhov, Gorky enjoyed a less than ideal association with Stanislavsky and Nemirovich-Danchenko. They rejected both his *Summer Visitors* (1904) and *Barbarians* (1906), whilst *Children of the Sun* went on in 1905 only after violent disagreement during rehearsals; following the Moscow armed rising in December it was

* Letter to Sumbatov-Yuzhin, 26 February 1903.

dropped as well. Thereafter twenty-nine years elapsed before the Moscow Art Theatre returned to Gorky.

In terms of theatre style the years leading up to 1917 were crucial in the development of the Russian theatre, witnessing the emergence of the great innovators, Meyerhold, Tairov, Evreinov and Vakhtangov. But in terms of content it was above all a period of retreat in the face of a censor grown sensitive to the point of paranoia and a theatre public reluctant to admit reality; it was an age of escapism – into the past, into fantasy, into exoticism, into pastiche and parody; it was the last antic fling of the World of Art.

Arrested in January for his deep involvement in the disaster of Bloody Sunday, Gorky wrote *Children of the Sun* during his imprisonment in the Peter and Paul Fortress in Petersburg. Shortly after his release in March he began work on *Enemies*. He had been in close contact with the revolutionary Social Democratic Party since December 1902 and the play's action reflects his familiarity with the pattern of disturbances in industry such as those at the Briansk metallurgical plant cited by Kvach in Act Three. More particularly Gorky was inspired by events early in 1905 at the huge Morozov textile plant in Orekhovo-Zuyevo.

The play was completed in August 1906 towards the end of Gorky's tour of America and published in December in Stuttgart and Petersburg. Some years earlier the censor had issued a directive explicitly forbidding the performance of plays dealing with industrial unrest, so there was no possibility of *Enemies* passing scrutiny. In February 1907 it was rejected with the following comments:

These scenes present a clear picture of the irreconcilable enmity between workers and employers, with the former portrayed as resolute fighters advancing clear-sightedly towards their declared aim of the overthrow of capital, and the latter shown as narrow-minded egotists. Furthermore, in the words of one of the characters, it is immaterial what kind of a man the boss is, it is enough that he is 'the boss' for him to be the enemy of the workers. The author . . . forecasts victory for the workers. These scenes are an outright provocation against the ruling classes and therefore cannot be authorized for performance.*

* Quoted in *Teatralnoe nasledie-1*, Leningrad 1934, p.223.

Six months later the published text was suppressed as well, but not before a production in the Ukraine and another in Central Asia had somehow escaped the authorities' notice. Before that on 16 February 1907 the play had been given its world première by Max Reinhardt at his Kleines Theater in Berlin. In 1903 Reinhardt had scored a memorable success with *The Lower Depths* which ran for over five-hundred performances, but *Enemies* proved far less popular. Commenting on this Plekhanov wrote:

> Whereas a well-portrayed tramp (of the Lumpenproletariat) may appeal to the bourgeois art-lover, a well-portrayed *politically conscious worker* is bound to provoke all kinds of most unpleasant thoughts. And as regards the Berlin proletariat, they have had little time for the theatre this winter.*

Despite the theatre's neglect of his plays Gorky continued throughout his exile on Capri to give dramatic shape to his preoccupation with the just and inevitable collapse of Russian society. Between 1908 and 1915 he wrote a further seven or eight plays devoted to various aspects of this theme including *Vassa Zheleznova*, the first dramatic adaptation of his novel *The Mother*, which in 1911 was awarded the Griboyedov Prize by the Society of Russian Dramatists. However there were no significant productions in Russia of his new works and most of them were not seen at all until after the Revolution.

In the early years of the Soviet period the Moscow Art Theatre was not alone in neglecting all his work but *The Lower Depths*. The opinion that it was outmoded and untheatrical persisted until after his final return in 1931. Two years earlier the first Five-Year Plan had been announced and at the same time the Party had taken measures to ensure far closer control of the arts and to eliminate the so-called 'leftist' deviations of the relatively permissive N.E.P. period. Theatre censorship was placed in the hands of a new Central Repertoire Committee or 'Glavrepertkom' and each theatre's artistic policy was subject to the control of a Party-dominated 'Artistic Council'. As a result many theatres reluctant to compromise their artistic standards were confronted with a repertoire crisis. For example, in the two seasons from 1930 to 1932 the Moscow Art

* Quoted in M. Gorky, *Polnoe sobranie sochinenii* – VIII, Moscow 1970, p. 677.

Theatre and Tairov's Kamerny Theatre succeeded in putting on only three new productions each. The position became more critical still in 1934 when at the inaugural congress of the new Writers' Union Zhdanov formulated the stifling principles of Socialist Realism and laid down the guide-lines for the elimination of formalism. Alone amongst leading directors Meyerhold refused to yield and within four years his theatre was liquidated, having added only one further production to its repertoire.

In these coercive circumstances the Soviet theatre began its reappraisal of Gorky the dramatist, stimulated in 1932 by the appearance of *Yegor Bulychov and Others*, one of a trilogy of plays set against the background of events from 1917 up to 1930.* A complex, often bizarre tragedy, *Yegor Bulychov* deals with a wealthy provincial merchant alienated from his own class and struggling for understanding as he dies of cancer during the last days of the Romanov dynasty. Encouraged by Boris Zakhava's vivid production at the Moscow Vakhtangov Theatre, directors started to look afresh at Gorky's earlier works. The following year within a single month there were revivals of *Enemies* at the Pushkin Theatre in Leningrad and at the Maly and the Trade Union Theatre in Moscow. Gorky's position in the Soviet repertoire was confirmed finally in October 1935 by the production of *Enemies* at the Moscow Art Theatre by Nemirovich-Danchenko and Mikhail Kedrov; it was performed 275 times and was taken to the Paris International Exhibition in 1937.

For the 1933 production Gorky extensively revised *Enemies*, aiming principally to reduce the audience's sympathy for the Bardins, to raise the political consciousness of Levshin, and to shift some emphasis away from Nadya and onto the workers.† But it was the times rather than the text that demanded these 'improvements'. David Jones's production at the Aldwych amply demonstrated the continuing relevance and theatricality of *Enemies* – meanwhile there remain at least fifteen other plays by Gorky which the English-speaking theatre has yet to discover.

EDWARD BRAUN

* The other two were *Somov and Others* (1931, published posthumously) and *Dostigayev and Others* (1932).
† See p. xvii below.

Preface: The 1971 Translation

Enemies is set in the garden, and then the house, of a country estate in provincial Russia. At the bottom of the garden is a river; beyond the river the strips of land where the peasants, once serfs belonging to the estate, unprofitably toil to scratch a bare living and pay their rent to the Bardin family, whose members have an affectionate but essentially callous relationship with them. Off to one side, hidden from the house by a row of trees, is a small textile factory, developed, probably, by the Bardins' father to help support the declining economy of the estate. Somewhere beyond the factory is the huddle of small houses where the workers live – a closed world to the Bardins.

It is the long, hot summer of 1905, when the whole of Russia was trembling on the edge of revolution, following the tragic massacre of a peaceful demonstration, known as 'Bloody Sunday', in January. Before the autumn was over a nine-day general strike was virtually to paralyse the country; paper concessions were to be forced from the Tsar by pressure from a briefly triumphant workers' Soviet; and the autocracy was to so far lose control of events that the German Kaiser saw fit to offer the Tsar asylum in his own country. It was not until the year's end that ruthless police measures were able to force the genie of social discontent back into its archaic confinement.

Gorky was deeply involved in all these events; was imprisoned after 'Bloody Sunday', when his apartment was used as a refuge by the workers' leaders; and, in December, was forced into exile. *Enemies* was written the following year when, after a fund-raising tour of America on behalf of the Bolsheviks, Gorky finally settled on Capri. Possibly because he had already experienced the censor's refusal to license one of his plays, there is no overt reference to these public events in the text of *Enemies*; but in the social situation which is the context of the play all the confused attitudes and simmering emotions which lay behind the 1905 disturbances are brought into sharp focus. Here we can see something of that seven-eighths of the iceberg of discontent which the Russian bourgeoisie hoped would melt away if only the visible one-eighth could be forced to submerge.

The social and economic position of the Bardin family typifies the bewildering changes which had overtaken society in the past half century. It was only just over forty years since the emancipation of the serfs, an act which, though overdue, had as its first result a further reduction in the standard of living of the peasants, and which accelerated the breaking up of the great agricultural estates. (Russia, not following the European practice of primogeniture, had been splitting up its estates into smaller and smaller parcels for generations.) Encouraged by the government's new policy of rapid industrialization, many landed families had, like the Bardins, founded factories on their estates in order to prop up their failing fortunes. But the new breed of workers, men like Grekov and Ryabtsov in *Enemies*, could not be treated with the paternal indifference to which the peasants were resigned; nor could the new breed of managers, men like Mikhail Skrobotov, be relied upon to behave like 'gentlemen' in their dealings with the workers.

But while, in the course of the nineteenth century, the number of industrial enterprises in Russia had increased from about 2,000 to something over 40,000, no corresponding extension of middle-class power had taken place to check the excesses of the autocracy, which exercised its totalitarian rule directly through its highly organized police forces. Thus, whenever the conditions of the new class of industrial workers led to outbreaks of discontent, there could be no appeal before 'the law' for justice or redress because, as the old soldier, Kon, says: 'There isn't any law. There's only orders.' And it was always the police, finally, who gave the orders.

In such a situation, well-meaning, muddled liberals like Zakhar Bardin were lost and powerless; practical managers like Mikhail Skrobotov were driven to increasingly tough, police-supported methods of enforcing their will; intellectuals who could see what was happening became, according to temperament, either revolutionaries, as Nadya surely did, or cynical wasters, like Yakov Bardin; and the workers, seeing no hope of improvement coming from the middle-classes, were driven to organizing themselves into illegal unions, ripe for the revolutionary message brought to them in pamphlets and discussion groups by a variety of socialist organizations. And yet, so determined were the Russian bourgeoisie not to see what was happening under their noses, that Paulina Bardin, hearing the word 'socialism', could laugh: 'Socialism! What, here, at the back of beyond? How comical!'

But *Enemies* is a social rather than a political play. Gorky was too good a writer, and too imbued with the poetic realism of Chekhov, whom he deeply admired, to narrow his art down to the purely polemical. However committed he was to the cause of the underdog, he never forgot that the oppressors were also human beings, vulnerable and confused, as much victims of history as those they oppressed. It was society itself that Gorky put up for trial, not the individuals trapped in their roles within it. For this reason, in approaching rehearsals for the RSC production of the play, David Jones, the director, took pains to ensure that every member of the cast, and everyone involved in the production, should first of all absorb as much as possible of the social background of the country and the period. The first week of rehearsals was spent entirely in watching, and subsequently discussing, films about or connected with life in Russia in the first decade of this century; the second week in reading and discussing histories, memoirs, volumes of letters, anything that might help us penetrate the minds of Gorky's characters and the social pressures to which they were subject. By the time the first rehearsals took place a common body of knowledge and understanding had been built up which proved an invaluable touchstone as the shape of the production began gradually to emerge.

There is no direct parallel in this country to the position of the workers on the Bardin estate. The closest we could come was to think of those isolated north country areas, still basically rural, where the development of a single industry, a coal mine perhaps, or a cotton mill, transformed the social structure within a generation. They remained cut off from the great conurbations, and the older workers, like Levshin in *Enemies*, retained something of the pride and independence of the farmers and craftsmen they sprang from, as well as a last trace of that 'human' relationship between master and man on which the feudal system prided itself.

It was with such an – admittedly tenuous – connection in mind that, when preparing this translation, we decided to give the speech of the workers an unemphasized northern rhythm. Demotic speech is always a problem in translation: too emphatic a parallel never carries conviction, while an anonymous, unplaced standard English is totally lifeless. But by finding speech patterns and rhythms which are characteristic of a specific area not too unlike the play's original setting, it is possible to give actors living dialogue to work with, without requiring them to develop broad, and probably inconsistent, accents.

The Russian text used for this translation was the original one of 1906. Gorky revised the play for its first production in Russian in 1933, in most instances for the worse. At the end of the play, for instance, one of the workers is made to round on Nadya and tell her that she couldn't possibly understand anything that was going on. This was 'necessary' because, in the orthodox Soviet view of history, no member of the bourgeoisie could ever have understood or sympathized with the workers' cause – as Nadya has been seen to do in the course of the play. Since Gorky, throughout his life, believed passionately in the special ability of young people to view the world through eyes unblemished by their own past compromises, it seems very likely that this, and other small but significant alterations, were inspired by the official cultural policy of the day.

In most cases, then, the 1933 revisions have been ignored. They were followed, however, in the removal of two minor and unnecessary characters; and a few lines of the 1933 text were 'borrowed' to help in the staging of the final curtain. These lines appear in italics. Elsewhere in the text, square brackets, [thus,] indicate cuts which were made in the RSC production, in most cases purely for reasons of length; and bold round brackets, (thus,) additions and emendations made to Gorky's text in order to clarify or give impact to a particular point.

We have used the shorter form of the patronymic, 'Ivanich', 'Dmitrevna', rather than the longer 'Ivanovich', 'Dmitriyevna', since in 1906 the only classes who would have used the latter form in speech would have been bureaucrats and the petty bourgeoisie. In *Enemies* the only characters to use the pedantic form are the clerk Pologgy and the Captain of Gendarmes, Boboyedov.

It was thought that the usual translation of the title of the police force to which Boboyedov belongs, the Corps of Gendarmes, might have confusing connotations for an English audience, and the phrase 'Security Corps' was chosen as more evocative of their real function. The Gendarmerie was a military force, founded in 1836 to give teeth to the newly-created 'Third Department', charged by Tsar Nicholas I with responsibility for State security. It was more integrated into society than the dreaded secret police, the *Okhrana*, but also more feared than the civil police, for it had almost limitless powers of arrest and interrogation without trial, and was responsible only to the Third Department's successor, the Ministry of the Interior. This explains why, in *Enemies*, although the Assistant Prosecutor, Nikolai Skrobotov, could boss the local police about as much as he liked, he is obliged to treat the stupid Captain Boboyedov with some deference, even to persuading him that he is the originator of Skrobotov's own strategies. And when young Nadya challenges the Captain's blind devotion to 'the Law', although Boboyedov treats the matter lightly they both know that she is being foolhardy. His joking riposte, 'Dear me. Well, in that case I'm afraid we'll have to send you to gaol. Arrest you and straight off to gaol with you!' carries a genuine threat. He could do it, and no one between the Bardin estate and St Petersburg could stop him.

One of the Gendarmerie's functions was to act as theatre censors. Gorky had already been refused a licence once, with his play *The Philistines*, and it was to happen again with *Enemies*. For a Russian audience of that time Boboyedov's remark to Tatiana, an actress, that his Corps were 'the true connoisseurs of art' would carry a very special flavour. For an English and – perhaps even more – American audience of today, what the play loses from our missing such immediate references is more than made up for by the light thrown forward into the darker corners of our own society.

JEREMY BROOKS

The British première of Enemies *was given by the Royal Shakespeare Company on 22nd July, 1971 at the Aldwych Theatre with the following cast:*

The Bardin Household

ZAKHAR BARDIN	Philip Locke
PAULINA, *his wife*	Brenda Bruce
YAKOV BARDIN, *his brother*	John Wood
TATIANA, *Yakov's wife*	Helen Mirren
NADYA, *Paulina's niece*	Mary Rutherford
GENERAL PECHENEGOV, *retired, the Bardins'*	
uncle	Sebastian Shaw
KON, *his batman*	Reg Lye
MIKHAIL SKROBOTOV, *Zakhar's business partner*	Patrick Stewart
KLEOPATRA, *Mikhail's wife*	Sara Kestelman
NIKOLAI SKROBOTOV, *his brother, assistant public*	
prosecutor	Alan Howard
AGRAFENA, *the housekeeper*	Lila Kaye
POLOGGY, *a clerk*	Phillip Manikum
SINTSOV, *a clerk*	Ben Kingsley
GREKOV	Glynne Lewis
LEVSHIN	David Waller
YAGODIN	Hugh Keays Byrne
RYABTSOV	Paul Alexander
YAKIMOV	Terence Taplin
FIRST WORKER	Patrick Godfrey
SECOND WORKER	Ronald Forfar
VYRIPAEV	John Kane
PEASANT WOMEN	Mary Allen
	Holly Wilson
CAPTAIN BOBOYEDOV, *Intelligence Corps*	Barry Stanton
KVACH, *his corporal*	Ralph Cotterill
LIEUTENANT STREPETOV, *Infantry Corps*	John York
DISTRICT POLICE INSPECTOR	Clement McCallin
POLICEMAN	Edward Phillips
SOLDIERS	Colin Edwynn
	Michael Egan

Directed by David Jones
Designed by Timothy O'Brien
Costumes by Tazeena Firth and Timothy O'Brien

The American première of Enemies *was given by the Repertory Theater of Lincoln Center on November 8, 1972 at the Vivian Beaumont Theater with the following cast:*

The Bardin Household

ZAKHAR BARDIN	Robert Symonds
PAULINA, *his wife*	Frances Sternhagen
YAKOV BARDIN, *his brother*	Joseph Wiseman
TATIANA, *Yakov's wife*	Nancy Marchand
NADYA, *Paulina's niece*	Susan Sharkey
GENERAL PECHENEGOV, *retired, the Bardins' uncle*	Stefan Schnabel
KON, *his orderly*	Will Lee
MIKHAIL SKROBOTOV, *Zakhar's business partner*	Philip Bosco
KLEOPATRA, *Mikhail's wife*	Barbara Cook
NIKOLAI SKROBOTOV, *his brother, assistant public prosecutor*	Josef Sommer
AGRAFENA, *the housekeeper*	Jane Rose
POLOGGY, *a clerk*	George Pentecost
SINTSOV, *a clerk*	Christopher Walken
GREKOV	Robert Phalen
LEVSHIR	Sydney Walker
YAGODIN	Fred Morsell
RYABTSOV $\Big\}$ *Workmen*	Everett McGill
YAKIMOV	Dan Sullivan
VYRIPAEV	Frank Dwyer
PEASANT WOMEN	Penelope Allen
	Murrell Gehman
	Carole Ocwieja
CAPTAIN BOBOYEDOV, *Intelligence Corps*	Tom Lacy
KVACH, *his corporal*	Ray Fry
LIEUTENANT STREPETOV, *Army Corps*	George Taylor
DISTRICT POLICE INSPECTOR	Louis Turenne
POLICEMAN	James Ray Weeks

Directed by Ellis Rabb
Settings by Douglas W. Schmidt
Lighting by John Gleason
Costumes by Ann Roth
Music Composed by Cathy MacDonald

ENEMIES

Act One

A garden. Tall, ancient lime trees. Beneath them, upstage, a white army tent. Right, under the trees, a wide couch made of turf with a table in front of it. Left, in the shade of the lime trees, a long table set for breakfast. A small samovar is boiling. Round the table are wicker chairs and armchairs. AGRAFENA *is making coffee.* KON *is standing under a tree, smoking his pipe.* POLOGGY *is in front of him.*

POLOGGY (*gesturing absurdly*). Of course, you know best. I am what you might call a small man, my life is totally insignificant it's true, but all the same every one of those cucumbers was grown by me with my own two hands and I simply cannot permit them to be picked without my getting some remuneration.

KON (*gloomily*). Nobody's asking your permission. They pick them, they'll go on picking them.

POLOGGY (*hands pressed to heart*). Oh, but look here, surely if one's property is being violated one has the right to ask for the protection of the law?

KON. You can ask. Today they're lopping cucumbers, tomorrow they'll be lopping heads. That's your law for you.

POLOGGY. Well, indeed, that's a peculiar thing to hear, coming from you, in fact a very dangerous thing! How can you, an ex-soldier, with medals on your chest, speak disrespectfully about the law?

KON. There isn't any law. There's only orders. Left turn! By the right, quick march! And away you go. When they shout Halt! – you stop.

AGRAFENA. Kon, I wish you wouldn't smoke that shag around here, it's enough to burn the leaves off the trees.

POLOGGY. If they only did it from hunger, I could understand, hunger can explain practically anything, in fact you might even say that all wicked actions are committed to satisfy hunger. When a person simply has to have food, then of course . . .

KON. Angels don't eat, but that didn't stop Satan setting himself against God.

POLOGGY (*delighted*). Now that's what I call real insolence!

> *Enter* YAKOV BARDIN. *He always has a guilty smile; his movements are apathetic and slow; his eyes sick and dull. He talks quietly, and as if he were listening closely to his own words.* POLOGGY *bows to him.* KON *straightens up and salutes smartly.*

YAKOV. Well? What?

POLOGGY. I've come to see Zakhar Ivanovich with a humble request . . .

AGRAFENA. He's come complaining. Some lads from the factory have been stealing his cucumbers.

YAKOV. Ah. Well, you'll have to tell my brother, not me.

POLOGGY. Perfectly correct. And I am in point of fact on my way to him this very moment . . .

KON (*irritably*). You're not on your way anywhere, you're just standing on one spot and whining.

POLOGGY. I fail to see how I am being a nuisance to you, Kon. If you'd been reading a newspaper, of course, something of that sort, then perhaps you might have been able to accuse me of . . .

YAKOV. Kon – here a moment.

KON (*crossing to* YAKOV). You're an old blabbermouth, Pologgy, always full of stupid complaints.

POLOGGY. You've absolutely no right to say things like that! What were we given tongues for, if not for submitting complaints?

AGRAFENA. Oh, do stop, Pologgy. You're more like a mosquito than a man.

YAKOV (*to* KON). What's he here for? Why can't he go away?

POLOGGY (*to* AGRAFENA). If my words offend your ear and fail to reach your heart, I shall be silent.

POLOGGY *saunters off, and as he goes along the path he feels the trees with his hand.*

YAKOV (*embarrassed*). Well, Kon? It seems I . . . offended someone again yesterday?

KON (*grinning wryly*). Does seem that way.

YAKOV (*walking up and down*). Hm. Extraordinary. Why am I always rude when I'm drunk?

KON. It's often the way . . . But some people are better drunk than sober.[We had a corporal in our company, he was a real creep when he was sober, a bully he was, and a squealer, but when he was drunk he'd cry like a baby. Brothers, he'd say, I'm only a man, same as you lot – come on, spit in my face. Some of them would, too.]

YAKOV. Who did I talk to yesterday?

KON. The prosecutor. You told him he had a mouth like a mousetrap . . .* Oh, but first off you got Zakhar Ivanich embarrassed...

YAKOV (*thoughtfully*). I always start on my brother first.

KON. Then it was the prosecutor. You told him the managing director's wife has a string of lovers.

YAKOV. Ah yes, I see. What's it to me, all that?

KON. Don't know, sir. And then you told . . .

YAKOV. All right, all right, Kon, that'll do. [I don't want to find I insulted everybody.] Ah, it's a dreadful thing, this vodka . . .

He goes over to the table, looks at the bottles, pours out a large glass of drink, sips it. AGRAFENA glances sideways at him, sighs.

I'm talking about my illness, Agrafena [Ivanovna]. You feel rather sorry for me, don't you?

AGRAFENA. Very sorry, Yakov Ivanich. You're so straight with everyone, just as if you weren't a gentleman at all.

YAKOV. But Kon here isn't sorry for anyone. He is a philosopher.

---

* Lit. Rus: '. . . a wooden tongue . . .'

It's people who've taken a beating who develop a philosophy. For a soldier to start thinking, he's got to have taken many a good beating – right, Kon?

The GENERAL *calls from the tent* – 'Hi! Kon!'.

You've been given a rough time, that's why you're so clever.

KON (*walking off*). One glimpse of the general, though, and I turn into a fool again.

GENERAL (*emerging from the tent*). Kon! Swimming! At the double, now!

They disappear down the garden. YAKOV *sits down and rocks on the chair.*

YAKOV. Is my wife still asleep?

AGRAFENA. Madame's up and has had a bathe.

YAKOV. So you feel sorry for me.

AGRAFENA. You should have treatment, sir.

YAKOV. Pour me a drop of brandy, then. I know there's some there.

AGRAFENA. You'd mebbe best not, Yakov Ivanich.

YAKOV. Why? One less drink isn't going to help, is it?

AGRAFENA *sighs and pours out a large glass of brandy.* MIKHAIL SKROBOTOV *enters, walking quickly, agitated. He rubs his black, pointed beard irritably, and twiddles his hat in his hand.*

MIKHAIL. Is Zakhar Ivanich up yet? No? Of course not. Give me . . . is there some cold milk? Thank you. Good morning, Yakov Ivanich. You want to hear the news? Those wretches are demanding that I sack Dichkov, the foreman . . . *demanding*! They threaten to stop work if I don't, damn them!

YAKOV. Well, sack him then.

MIKHAIL. Oh yes, very simple – but that's not the point. The point is, Yakov Ivanich, that concessions are bad for discipline. Today it's only sacking the foreman, tomorrow they'll be wanting my head on a plate.

YAKOV (*gently*). You think they'll wait for tomorrow.

MIKHAIL. Very funny, I'm sure. But just you try dealing with those grubby gentlemen, all two thousand of them, with their heads turned by your brother, will all his liberal nonsense, as well as by all kinds of idiots with their stupid leaflets. . . . (*Looks at his watch.*) Nearly ten o'clock, and they're promising to start their nonsense after lunch . . . I must say, Yakov Ivanich, your dear brother has certainly ruined the factory for me while I've been away, the men have been completely corrupted by his lack of firmness.

YAKOV. You must tell him that.

MIKHAIL. I've told him once and I shall tell him again.

AGRAFENA. Here comes Paulina Dmitrevna.

YAKOV. That means they'll all appear.

> *Enter* SINTSOV, *right. He is about thirty, looks wary, often smiles. In his bearing and face there is something calm and distinctive.*

SINTSOV. Mikhail Vassilich, there are some workers' representatives in the office. They're demanding to see the managing director.

MIKHAIL. Demanding, are they? Tell them to go to hell.

> PAULINA *has entered, right.*

I beg your pardon, Paulina Dmitrevna.

PAULINA (*amiably*). You're always swearing. What is it this time?

MIKHAIL. What is it? It's your 'proletariat', as usual! Now they come *demanding*! They used to come begging for things, humbly. But now it's 'demand'!

PAULINA. You're very hard with the men, I must say.

MIKHAIL (*raising his arms and then letting them drop in a despairing gesture*). Well, really!

SINTSOV. What am I to tell the men in the office?

MIKHAIL. Tell them to wait. Go on, then.

SINTSOV *walks off, without hurrying.*

PAULINA. He has an interesting face, that clerk. Has he been with us long?

MIKHAIL. About a year.

PAULINA. He gives the impression of being a superior type [of person]. Who is he?

MIKHAIL (*shrugs*). [A clerk. Not a bad worker.] Earns forty roubles a month. (*He looks at his watch, sighs, looks round, sees* POLOGGY *under the tree.*) Well? What is it?

POLOGGY. I've come to see Zakhar Ivanovich, sir.

MIKHAIL. What for?

POLOGGY. On account, sir, of an infringement of the laws of property.

MIKHAIL (*to* PAULINA). Allow me to introduce another of our new clerks, a man of remarkable gifts – he has a passion for growing vegetables. He also harbours a deep conviction that everything on earth was created expressly to infringe his interests. Everything's against him – the sun, England, new machinery, the frogs . . .

POLOGGY (*smiling*). If I may make so bold, sir, when the frogs start up their croaking they bother everybody.

MIKHAIL. Get on back to the office! What do you think you're doing, dropping your work all the time to come up here complaining? I don't like it – go on, away with you!

POLOGGY *bows and goes off.* PAULINA *watches him through her lorgnette, smiling.*

PAULINA. There, you see how strict you are. And he's quite amusing, really. You know, I'm sure Russians are much more diverse than people abroad.

MIKHAIL. If you said, much more perverse, I'd agree with you. I've been in management for fifteen years now, and I assure you I know all there is to know about your noble Russian working man. Just to think of them makes my head spin and my stomach heave. Oh, what's keeping Zakhar Ivanich!

PAULINA (*to* AGRAFENA). Grusha, go and call my husband. (*To* MIKHAIL.) You know what he's doing? He's finishing off yesterday's game of chess with your brother.

MIKHAIL. Naturally. And meanwhile the workers are planning to go on strike after lunch. I tell you, Russia will never come to any good. It's a fact. This is a country of anarchists. Work-shy anarchists. There's an ingrown revulsion for work ... an utter incapacity for order ... total lack of respect for the law.

PAULINA. But of course! How can there be respect for the law in a country that has no laws? I mean, between you and me, our government ...

MIKHAIL. Oh, I'm not trying to justify anyone! The government's as riddled with anarchy as anyone else. Now the Anglo-Saxon – he's the law's punch-bag.

Enter, behind, ZAKHAR BARDIN *and* NIKOLAI SKROBOTOV.

There's no better material for building a state. Your Englishman dances along in front of the law like a circus horse on its hind legs, he's got respect for the law built into his very bone and muscle ... Ah, here they are. Good morning, Zakhar Ivanich. Morning, Nikolai. (*To* ZAKHAR.) May I tell you the latest result of your liberal policies with the workers? They're demanding I sack Dichkov immediately. If I don't, they stop work. So – how about that?

ZAKHAR (*rubbing his forehead*). Hm ... Yes ... Dichkov? Isn't he the one who's always fighting? Some story about girls, too? Yes, yes, I know him. Well, yes, by all means dismiss him, it would only be just.

MIKHAIL (*agitated*). Oh, really, Zakhar Ivanich! With all due respect to you as my partner and colleague, can't we talk seriously? It's a question of good business practice, not of justice – justice is Nikolai's affair, not ours. And I'm sorry but I must tell you again that your idea of justice is the ruination of good business.

ZAKHAR. Oh, come now, you're talking in paradoxes!

MIKHAIL. The paradox is the idea of justice in industry, can't you understand?

NIKOLAI. You're shouting, Mikhail.

PAULINA. Talking business in front of me, and so early in the morning! It's not very polite.

MIKHAIL. I'm sorry, Paulina Dmitrevna, but I have to. It seems to me absolutely vital to make this clear. Until I went away on leave I held the factory like *that* – (*He holds up a clenched fist.*) – and no one dared let out so much as a squeak. As you know, I considered all these Sunday classes – reading circles and so on – unwise in the kind of situation we have here. When the raw Russian brain is touched with the spark of knowledge it doesn't burst into the light of reason, it simply smoulders and stinks and . . . I'm sorry, I seem to be digressing.

NIKOLAI. You should talk a little more quietly.

MIKHAIL (*hardly able to control himself*). Thank you for the advice, Nikolai, no doubt it's very sound but it doesn't happen to suit me. In a mere six months, Zakhar Ivanich, your treatment of the workers has shaken and undermined the entire structure which it took me eight years of hard work to build! They respected me, they regarded me as the master. But now it's perfectly clear that there are two masters, one kind and one cruel. The kind one, of course, is you . . .

ZAKHAR (*embarrassed*). Oh, really, why talk like that?

PAULINA. You are saying some odd things, Mikhail Vassilich.

MIKHAIL. I've every reason to. I've been put in an idiotic position. Last time this came up I told the workers I'd close the factory rather than dismiss Dichkov. They realized I meant what I said, and calmed down. Then on Friday, Zakhar Ivanich, in the canteen, you told that man Grekov that Dichkov was a ruffian and that you intended to sack him.

ZAKHAR (*gently*). But my dear chap, if he goes around striking men on the jaw . . . and all that? Surely we can't allow that sort of thing? We're Europeans, we're civilized people.

MIKHAIL. First and foremost, we're factory owners. Every holiday the workers go around bashing each other on the jaw – what's it got to do with us? [Anyway, you'll have to put off teaching them good manners for the moment.] There's a deputation waiting for you in the office; they're going to demand the dismissal of Dichkov. What do you intend to do?

ZAKHAR. But surely Dichkov isn't all that valuable? I'm sure he's not, you know . . .

NIKOLAI (*coldly*). It seems to me it's not so much a question of the man, as of the principle.

MIKHAIL. Exactly. The question is, who are the masters in this factory – you and I, or the workers?

ZAKHAR (*at a loss*). I understand that, but . . .

MIKHAIL. If we give in to them on this, what will they demand next? They're brazen. Six months of Sunday reading circles and all the rest of the Europeanism have done their stuff – they glare at me like wolves. And then there's these leaflets going around . . . it all smacks of socialism to me, I don't mind saying.

PAULINA. Socialism! What, here, at the back of beyond? How comical!

MIKHAIL. Comical? Perhaps it is, to you. My dear Paulina Dmitrevna, all children are amusing while they're young and small. But bit by bit they grow up, until one day you find yourself facing full-grown scoundrels.

ZAKHAR. What do you want to do, then?

MIKHAIL. Close down the factory. Let them go hungry for a bit – that'll cool them down.

YAKOV *gets up, goes over to the table, has a drink, and walks slowly off, left.*

[Closing the factory will involve the women. They'll start weeping. Women's tears act like smelling salts on men drunk with dreams. They soon sober up.]

PAULINA. You're talking very ruthlessly, Mikhail Vassilich.

MIKHAIL. Certainly. Life demands it.

ZAKHAR. But, look, are you sure this is . . . is it really unavoidable? I mean, it seems so . . .

MIKHAIL. Have you something else to suggest?

ZAKHAR. Well – I could go and talk to them, couldn't I?

MIKHAIL. You'd only give in to them, and make my position even more impossible. No, I'm sorry, but I find you and your promises offensive as well as harmful.

ZAKHAR (*hurriedly*). Oh, I'm not arguing, my dear chap! I'm just wondering what's for the best. I'm more of a country gentleman than an industrialist, you know, and all this is new to me, and very difficult. I want to see justice done, but. . . . You know, the peasants are so much more gentle and good-natured than the workers, I've always got on splendidly with them. . . . Of course, there are some interesting characters among the workers, but on the whole I agree – they *are* awfully unruly . . .

MIKHAIL. [Particularly since you started handing out promises all round . . .

ZAKHAR. But don't you see, as soon as you left they started to get restless . . . I mean, there were agitations and . . . Well, perhaps I did behave unwisely, but I had to calm them down somehow, didn't I? We were being written about in the newspapers – written about critically, I mean . . .]

MIKHAIL (*impatiently*). It's now seventeen minutes past ten. We have to make a decision. There are two possibilities. Either I close the factory down – or I go. Closing the factory will cost us nothing, I've seen to that. The urgent orders are all ready, and there are reserves in the warehouses.

ZAKHAR. Hm, yes. I see. We have to decide, do we? Yes, yes, of course. Nikolai Vassilich, what do you think?

NIKOLAI. I can only talk about it in the abstract, but from that point of view, of course, my brother's right. If civilization means anything to us, we must stand firmly by our principles. A factory is a state in miniature.

MIKHAIL (*with a disparaging gesture*). You'll get yourself into trouble with that analogy.

NIKOLAI. Not at all. Every state has to have a governing body which can bind together the conflicting interests of its component parts with hoops of steel . . .

MIKHAIL. Is that out of a book?

NIKOLAI. . . . don't be so testy . . . and a body in power is only firmly in power when it holds its subjects strictly within the framework it has drawn up for them.

ZAKHAR. In other words, you agree we should close down? Oh dear . . . Mikhail Vassilich, don't be angry . . . I'll give you my answer in . . . ten minutes? All right?

MIKHAIL. Certainly.

ZAKHAR (*walking quickly off left*). Paulina, come with me, will you?

PAULINA (*following him*). Oh God, this is all so disturbing!

MIKHAIL (*through his teeth*). Spineless jellyfish!

NIKOLAI. Calm down, Mikhail. No need to lose all control.

MIKHAIL. Can't you understand? My nerves are completely shattered! I go down to the factory and – look! (*He takes a revolver out of his pocket.*) I'm not blind, and I'm not a fool. They hate me, thanks to that – imbecile! And I can't just abandon the business, you'd be the first to blame me if I did. Our entire capital is tied up in it. And if I pull out, that balding ditherer will ruin everything!

NIKOLAI (*calmly*). Hm, that's bad. Unless you're exaggerating.

SINTSOV (*entering*). The men are asking for you.

MIKHAIL. For me? What is it now?

SINTSOV. There's a rumour the factory's going to be closed after dinner.

MIKHAIL (*to his brother*). How about that? Who could have told them?

NIKOLAI. Probably Yakov Ivanich.

MIKHAIL. Oh, hell! (*He looks at SINTSOV, unable to disguise his irritation*.) Well, what concern is it of yours, Mr Sintsov? Coming out here, asking . . . . Eh? What?

SINTSOV. The book-keeper asked me to come and fetch you.

MIKHAIL. He did, eh? And what's this habit you've got of leering and smirking like that, eh? What are you so happy about, then?

SINTSOV. I think that's my own business.

MIKHAIL. Well I don't. And I strongly advise you to watch your conduct when you're with me. . . . Yes!

SINTSOV. May I go?

MIKHAIL. You may.

TATIANA *enters from the right.*

TATIANA. Aha, the managing director! In a hurry again? (*Calls out to* SINTSOV.) Good morning, Matvey Nikolaich.

SINTSOV (*warmly*). Good morning. How are you? I hope you're not too tired this morning!

TATIANA. Not at all. My arms ache a bit from all that rowing yesterday, that's all. You on your way to work? I'll come as far as the gate. Do you know what I want to say to you?

SINTSOV. How could I?

TATIANA (*walking beside* SINTSOV). There was a lot of sense in what you were saying yesterday, but the *way* you said it was too aggressive, too . . . prejudiced. Some things are far more convincing if you say them without too much emotion . . .

The rest of their conversation becomes inaudible.

MIKHAIL. Did you see that? Oh, it's impossible! One moment you're telling off an employee for being insolent, the next he's hobnobbing under your very eyes with the wife of your partner's brother. . . . The brother's a drunkard, the wife's an actress, and what the hell they're doing here nobody has any idea.

NIKOLAI. She's an odd woman. Good looking, dresses well, most attractive in fact – and yet she seems bent on having an affair with a pauper. Original, perhaps, but foolish.

MIKHAIL (*ironically*). It's called being democratic. She's the daughter of a laundress, you see, so she claims to feel happier among the common people.

NIKOLAI.... I've a notion she's quite approachable, too – seems to be the sensual type ... all right, you needn't gape like that!

MIKHAIL. What's happened to that liberal of ours? Gone back to sleep, I expect.... No, I tell you, what Russia lacks is vitality. The people are dazed, nobody knows his own place, they just wander about, dreaming and talking ... the whole thing's falling apart, it's all cock-eyed; there are hardly any people of real talent about, and if there are any, they're all anarchists. [The government's just a gang of crazed, angry, stupid men, unable to understand anything, unable to do anything. Instead of a Russian history all we get is the endless Russian scandal.] Above all, nobody takes the slightest interest in their work ...

NIKOLAI. You're talking the most extraordinary nonsense, you know.

MIKHAIL. What?

TATIANA (*returning*). Are you shouting too? Everyone's started to shout for some reason.

AGRAFENA. Mikhail Vassilich ... Zakhar Ivanich is asking if you'd ...

MIKHAIL. Ah, at last.

> MIKHAIL *exits without letting* AGRAFENA *finish her sentence.* TATIANA *sits down at the table.*

TATIANA. What's he so excited about?

NIKOLAI. I doubt if you'd find it interesting.

TATIANA (*calmly*). Possibly. You know, he reminds me of a policeman I once knew. We used to have this policeman on duty in the theatre in Kostroma – a tall man, with protruding eyes ...

NIKOLAI. I don't see the resemblance to my brother.

TATIANA. I'm not talking about physical resemblance. This policeman, he was always hurrying somewhere, too. He never walked, he ran. He didn't smoke, he practically asphyxiated himself. [He didn't seem to be living at all, he was so busy jumping and turning somersaults in an effort to attain something as quickly as possible – though he never knew what.

NIKOLAI. Are you sure he didn't?

TATIANA. Quite sure. Anyone with a clear purpose pursues it calmly. But he was in a perpetual hurry, and a very peculiar kind of hurry – it whipped him on from inside, so he ran and he ran and got in his own way and everyone else's too. He wasn't greedy, in the narrow sense, only greedily anxious to get all his duties behind him as quickly as possible, including the duty of taking bribes.] He didn't just take bribes, he snatched them, snatch and run off without even time to say thank you. In the end he was run over by some horses and killed.

NIKOLAI. Are you trying to say that my brother's efforts are all pointless?

TATIANA. Is that what it sounded like? I didn't mean that . . . it's just that he's like that policeman.

NIKOLAI. None of it very flattering to my brother.

TATIANA. I wasn't trying to flatter him.

NIKOLAI. You have a curious way of flirting.

TATIANA. Indeed?

NIKOLAI. It's rather depressing.

TATIANA (*calmly*). Don't some women find you depressing?

NIKOLAI. Ah-ha!

PAULINA (*entering*). Everything seems to be going wrong today, somehow. No one's had breakfast, they're all out of temper, you'd think they hadn't had enough sleep. Nadya went off into the woods early this morning, with Kleopatra Petrovna, to pick mushrooms – I told her not to only yesterday. Life is really getting too difficult!

TATIANA. You eat too much.

PAULINA. Really, Tanya, what's that tone for? Your attitude towards other people is quite abnormal.

TATIANA. Because it's calm?

PAULINA. Oh, it's easy enough to be calm when [you've got nothing, when] you're free of all responsibility! But when you've got thousands of people depending on you for food – I can tell you, it's no joke.

TATIANA. [Why not give it all up then? Stop feeding them, let them live how they like.] Give it all away, the factory, the land, everything. . . . And calm down.

PAULINA. How can you talk like that? You should see how upset Zakhar is. We've decided to close the factory for a while, until the workers have come to their senses. But don't you see how distressing it is? Hundreds of people will be out of work. A lot of them have children. It's terrible.

TATIANA. Don't do it then, if it's so terrible. Why cause yourself pain?

PAULINA. Oh, Tanya, you're maddening! If we don't close, the workers will strike, and that'll be even worse.

TATIANA. What will be worse?

PAULINA. Everything! We can't give in to their every demand, can we? Anyway, it's not their demands at all, it's those socialists, putting ideas in their heads and teaching them to shout. (*Vehemently – but obscurely : she has no idea what she's talking about.*) I can't understand it! Socialism abroad is perfectly appropriate, it makes life more various and it's all done out in the open. But here in Russia it gets whispered to the workers in holes and corners, regardless of the fact that in a monarchy it's quite out of place! What we need is a constitution, not that sort of thing. What do you think, Nikolai Vassilich?

NIKOLAI (*smiling*). A little differently. Socialism's a highly dangerous phenomenon. And in a country which has no philosophy of its own, no racial philosophy so to speak, where everyone grabs any ideas that are going around, it's bound to fall on fertile soil. We're a people of extremes. That's our sickness.

PAULINA. Oh, how true that is! Yes, we're a people of extremes.

TATIANA (*getting up*). Particularly you and your husband. Not to mention the assistant prosecutor here.

PAULINA. You don't know anything about it, Tanya. Zakhar is considered to be one of the reds of the province.

TATIANA (*walking up and down*). I should think he's only red with shame – and that not often.

PAULINA. Tanya! What *is* the matter with you, for God's sake?

TATIANA. Was that an insult? I didn't know. [To me, your life is like a play put on by amateurs. The parts have been wrongly cast, nobody's got a scrap of talent, everybody's acting abominably, so the play makes no sense at all.

NIKOLAI. There's something in that. . . . And everyone's complaining, 'Oh, what a boring play!'

TATIANA. That's right. We're ruining the play. And I think the extras and the stage hands are beginning to realize it. One day they'll just chase us off the stage . . .]

    Enter the GENERAL *and* KON.

NIKOLAI. Now wait a minute! What are you getting at?

GENERAL. (*shouting as he approaches*). Paulina! Milk for the general! Ha! *Cold* milk! (*To* NIKOLAI.) Aha, the tombstone of the Law! (*To* TATIANA.) My excellent niece – your hand! (*To* KON.) Kon, question one: what is a soldier?

KON (*drearily*). Whatever those in command wish him to be, your excellency.

GENERAL. Can he be a fish?

KON. A soldier must be able to do anything that . . .

TATIANA. Uncle dear, you amused us with this little scene yesterday. Surely you don't play it every day?

PAULINA (*with a sigh*). Every day, after his swim.

GENERAL. Yes, every day! And every day different, that's how it has to be done! This old clown has to think up the questions as well as the answers.

TATIANA. Do you enjoy that, Kon?

KON. The General enjoys it.

TATIANA. What about you?

GENERAL. He does too.

KON. I don't, really. I'm a bit old for circus acts. But if you want to eat you have to put up with it.

GENERAL. Oho, you cunning old rascal. About turn! Quick march! Left, right, left, right . . .

TATIANA. Don't you get bored with making a fool of an old man?

GENERAL. I'm an old man myself. And you bore me. Actresses are supposed to amuse people. What are you doing about that?

PAULINA. Uncle, did you know . . .

GENERAL. I don't know anything.

PAULINA. We're closing the factory.

GENERAL. Ah! Good idea! It *hoots*! There you are, sound asleep in the early morning, and suddenly – hoo-oo-oo-oot! Close it down, by all means.

   MIKHAIL *enters, walking fast.*

MIKHAIL. Nikolai, here a moment. Well, the factory's closed. But we'd better take some precautions, just in case. Get off a telegram to the vice-governor, tell him briefly how things stand, and ask for some troops. Put my name to it.

NIKOLAI. He's my friend, too.

MIKHAIL. I know. I'm off now to tell those damn delegates about the closure. Don't say a word about the telegram – I'll let them know myself when the moment comes, all right?

NIKOLAI. Yes.

MIKHAIL. You know, it really feels wonderful when you make a stand! It's a sign of youth. I may be older than you in years, Nikolai, but I'm younger in heart, eh?

NIKOLAI. I think it's less a question of youth than of being highly strung.

MIKHAIL (*ironically*). Oh yes, of course! Goodbye now. I'll show you who's highly strung, just you wait and see!

   MIKHAIL *exits, laughing.*

PAULINA. So it's decided then, is it, Nikolai Vassilich?

NIKOLAI (*exiting*). So it seems.

PAULINA. Oh my God!

GENERAL. What's been decided?

PAULINA. To close down the factory.

GENERAL. Oh, that. You already told me. Tra-lala. Te-te-tum. It's boring.

TATIANA. I agree.

PAULINA. But it's all so worrying and awkward!

GENERAL. Kon!

KON. Sir!

GENERAL. Rods. Boat. All correct?

KON. Ready and correct, sir.

GENERAL. I'm going to converse with the fish, since I'm averse to humans. (*He roars with laughter*.) Ha! Nicely put, eh? (*Enter* NADYA, *running*.) Ah, my little butterfly! What's up?

NADYA (*joyfully*). We've had an adventure! (*She turns back, and calls*.) Come on, do! Grab his arm, Kleopatra Petrovna! (*To* PAULINA) We were just coming out of the woods, Aunt Paulina, and suddenly [there were] these three drunken workers . . . (came up to us.)

PAULINA. There you are! Haven't I always told you . . . (not to wander in the woods!)

KLEOPATRA *enters*, GREKOV *behind her*.

KLEOPATRA. Just think how disgusting!

NADYA. Why disgusting? It was just funny! Three workers, aunt, all smiling and saying, 'Dear ladies, dear ladies . . .'

KLEOPATRA. I shall certainly ask my husband to dismiss them.

GREKOV (*smiling*). What for?

GENERAL (*to* NADYA). Who is that, under all the dirt?

NADYA. He's the one who rescued us, Grandfather, don't you understand?

GENERAL. I don't understand a thing.

KLEOPATRA (*to* NADYA). Nobody could, the way you tell it.

NADYA. I'm telling it perfectly well.

PAULINA. But, Nadya, we don't understand any of it.

NADYA. That's because you all keep interrupting! They came up to us and they said, 'Dear ladies, dear young ladies, let's all sing a song together . . .'

PAULINA. Oh! What an impertinence!

NADYA. No, no, it wasn't, really! They said, 'We know you sing very well. Of course, we have taken a drink,' they said, 'but we're all the better for that.' And it's true, Aunt Paulina, when they're a bit drunk they aren't as sullen as usual.

KLEOPATRA. Fortunately for us this young man . . .

NADYA. I can tell it better than you. And then Kleopatra Petrovna started to scold them – you shouldn't have done that, I'm sure you shouldn't. And then one of them, a tall, thin man . . .

KLEOPATRA (*grimly*). I happen to know his name.

NADYA. . . . took her arm and said, sadly, somehow, 'You're such a beautiful, well-educated woman, it's a real pleasure to look at you, and yet here you are swearing at us. We haven't harmed you, have we?' He said that so nicely, you know, right from the heart. And then one of the others, he was, well, really rather . . . He said, 'Why talk to them? They don't know anything. They're just wild beasts.' Us! Wild beasts!

 NADYA *laughs*.

TATIANA (*smiling*). You seem to like the label.

PAULINA. I warned you, Nadya. You're always running about all over the place . . .

GREKOV (*to* NADYA). May I go?

NADYA. Oh, no, please don't! Look, have some tea? Or some milk? Will you?

 The GENERAL *laughs.* KLEOPATRA *shrugs.* TATIANA *watches* GREKOV, *humming to herself.* PAULINA *lowers her head and carefully wipes a spoon with a cloth.*

GREKOV (*smiling*). No thank you. I won't have anything.

NADYA (*persuading*). Please. Don't be shy. (He's just an old man.)
They're all good, kind people, honestly!

PAULINA (*protesting*). Oh, Nadya!

NADYA [(*to* GREKOV). Don't go. I want to tell them the whole
story . . .

KLEOPATRA (*irritably*). In a word, this young man made a timely
appearance and persuaded his drunken friends to leave us in
peace. I asked him to escort us home and that was it.

NADYA. Oh no, how can you say that? If all that happened was
what you said, everyone would die of boredom!

GENERAL. By jove! Die of boredom, eh?]

NADYA (*to* GREKOV). Oh, do sit down! Aunt Paulina, ask him to
sit down. Why are you all looking so sour? Are you too hot, or
what?

PAULINA (*to* GREKOV). Thank you, young man.

GREKOV. It was nothing.

PAULINA (*more coldly*). It was good of you to defend these young
women.

GREKOV (*quietly*). They didn't need defending. No one was harm-
ing them.

NADYA. Oh, Aunt Paulina! How can you speak in that tone?

PAULINA. Please don't teach me how to speak.

NADYA. [But don't you understand, it wasn't a question of
defending! He just said, 'Leave off, lads! That's no way.' And
they were delighted to see him! 'Grekov!' they said, 'come on
then, you're a good lad!' And he really is good, Aunt Paulina,
and clever. . . . I'm sorry, Grekov, but you are, you know.

GREKOV (*grinning*). You're putting me in an awkward spot.

NADYA. Am I? I didn't mean to. . . . It's not me, it's them,
Grekov.

PAULINA. Nadya! I really don't understand these transports of
delight. It's all too absurd. That's enough, now.

NADYA (*excited*). Laugh, then, if I'm funny! Don't just sit there
like a lot of owls, go ahead and laugh!]

KLEOPATRA. Nadya has a way of turning every trifle into an

occasion for noisy ecstasies. And this is a fine time to choose, in front of a . . . stranger . . . who, as you see, is laughing at her.

NADYA (*to* GREKOV). Are you laughing at me?

GREKOV (*simply*). Not at all. I'm admiring you.

PAULINA (*astonished*). Oh, really! Uncle, please . . .

KLEOPATRA (*with a wry smile*). There you are, you see.

GENERAL. Now then, basta! The joke's gone far enough. Here, young man – here you are. Now be off with you.

GREKOV (*turning away*). Thank you. I don't want it.

NADYA (*covering her face*). Oh Grandfather! Why?

GENERAL (*stopping* GREKOV). Hold on! This is ten roubles!

GREKOV (*calmly*). What of it?

They are all silent for a moment.

GENERAL (*embarrassed*). Er . . . what, er . . . who are you?

GREKOV. A worker.

GENERAL. A blacksmith?

GREKOV. A fitter.

GENERAL (*severely*). Same thing. Why don't you take the money, eh?

GREKOV. I don't want to.

GENERAL (*irritated*). What are you playing at? What *do* you want?

GREKOV. Nothing.

GENERAL. Sure you don't want to ask for the young lady's hand, eh?

The GENERAL *roars with laughter; the others are embarrassed.*

NADYA. Oh! What are you *doing*!?

PAULINA. Uncle, please.

GREKOV (*calmly, to the* GENERAL). How old are you?

GENERAL (*surprised*). What? How old? Me?

GREKOV (*as before*). How old are you?

GENERAL (*glancing round*). What is this? Er, well – sixty-one. What of it?

GREKOV (*walking away*). At your age you should have more sense.

GENERAL. What's that? More sense? Me?

NADYA *runs after* GREKOV.

NADYA. Listen, please don't be angry. [He's an old man. They're all nice people, really.

GENERAL. What the devil . . . ?]

GREKOV. Don't worry yourself. It's all quite natural.

NADYA. [It's the heat, it puts them in a bad mood. And I didn't tell the story well at all . . .

GREKOV (*smiling*). However you told it, they wouldn't have understood, believe me.]

GREKOV *and* NADYA *exit together*.

GENERAL. How dare he talk to me like that!

TATIANA. You shouldn't have thrust your money at him.

PAULINA. Ah, Nadya! That Nadya!

KLEOPATRA. The nerve of it! Playing the proud spaniard like that! I shall certainly [see that] (ask) my husband . . . (to dismiss him!)

GENERAL. The young pup!

PAULINA. But, really, Nadya's impossible! And then to walk off with him! She really worries me.

KLEOPATRA. These 'Socialists' of yours get more impudent every day.

PAULINA. What makes you think he's a socialist?

KLEOPATRA. I can see it. All the superior workers are socialists!

GENERAL. I shall tell Zakhar. He can throw that young pup out of the factory on his neck.

TATIANA. The factory's closed.

GENERAL. Right out on his neck.

PAULINA. Tanya, call Nadya back, will you, dear? Tell her I'm – I'm deeply shocked.

TATIANA *goes out*.

GENERAL. The scoundrel. How old, eh?

KLEOPATRA. Those drunks *whistled* at us! (*To* PAULINA.) And you – you play along with them . . . All those reading circles . . . What's the point of it all?

PAULINA. Yes, yes . . . and on Thursday when I was driving through the village, imagine! Suddenly there was a whistle – they even whistle at me! Quite apart from the rudeness, they might have frightened the horses!

KLEOPATRA (*sententiously*). Zakhar Ivanich is much to blame. As my husband says, he doesn't keep a proper distance between himself and those people.

PAULINA. He's too gentle. He wants to be kind to everyone. He's convinced that a friendly relationship with the people is to the advantage of both sides, and certainly the peasants bear this out – they lease the land, pay their rents, and everything's fine. But these . . .

Enter TATIANA *and* NADYA.

Nadya, my dear! Don't you understand how improper . . .

NADYA (*passionately*). It's you, you who's improper! You're all out of your minds with the heat, you're vicious, and sick, and you don't understand anything! As for you, Grandfather – Oh, how *stupid* you are!

GENERAL (*furious*). Me? Stupid? How much more . . . ?

NADYA. Why did you have to say that . . . about asking for my hand? Aren't you ashamed of yourself?

GENERAL. Ashamed? No! No, basta! I've had enough for one day! (*He walks away and bellows.*) Kon! Where the devil are you? Got your feet stuck in the mud, have you? Idiot! Blockhead! (*He exits.*)

NADYA. And you, Aunt Paulina, you of all people! You've lived abroad, you talk about politics . . . not to invite him to sit down, not even to offer him a cup of tea – you . . . you grand lady, you!

PAULINA (*gets up and throws down the spoon*). No, this is frightful.

It's intolerable, [you don't know what you're saying.] (stop it at once.)

NADYA. And you too, Kleopatra Petrovna, you were polite as anything on the way back but as soon as we got here . . .

KLEOPATRA. Well, really, what was I supposed to do? Kiss him? I'm sorry, but his face was dirty. And I don't feel like listening to your reprimands, any more. . . . You see, Paulina Dmitrevna? There's your democracy for you – or – what d'you call it? – your humanism. For the moment my husband has to cope with it all, but you wait – it'll come back on you eventually.

PAULINA. Kleopatra Petrovna, I do apologize to you for Nadya . . .

KLEOPATRA (*leaving*). Quite unnecessary. It isn't only her. It's not just Nadya, you're all to blame . . .

KLEOPATRA *exits*.

PAULINA. Nadya – when your mother was dying and entrusted me with you and your upbringing . . .

NADYA. Leave Mama out of it! You get it all wrong when you talk about her!

PAULINA (*amazed*). Nadya! Are you ill? Pull yourself together. Your mother was my sister, I knew her better than you did.

NADYA (*in unrestrained tears*). You don't know anything! Poor people and rich people can never be sisters! My mother was poor, but she was good. You couldn't ever understand poor people, you don't even understand Aunt Tanya!

PAULINA. Nadya – I must ask you to leave us. Go along, please.

NADYA (*leaving*). Oh, I'll go. But I'm right all the same. It's me that's right, not you.

PAULINA. Good heavens! A perfectly healthy girl, and then suddenly she throws a fit like that! Almost hysterical. I'm sorry, Tanya, but I can see your influence at work here. It's true. [You talk to her about everything, just as if she was a grown-up. Taking her off to meet our employees, all those clerks – so-called working-class intellectuals – really, it's ludicrous! And taking her out boating with you . . .]

TATIANA. Oh, do calm down. Have a drink or something. You must agree your behaviour with that workman wasn't very sensible. Nothing would have happened to the chair if you'd asked him to sit on it.

PAULINA. No, you're wrong, you know. Nobody could say I treat the workers badly, but there's a limit to everything, my dear.

Enter YAKOV, *slowly, drunk.*

TATIANA. And whatever you say, I don't take her everywhere – she goes by herself. And I think she should be allowed to.

PAULINA. [She goes by herself! As if she understood where she's going!]

YAKOV (*sitting*). There's going to be a riot at the factory.

PAULINA (*wearily*). Oh, stop it, Yakov!

YAKOV. There is, you know. There'll be a riot. They'll burn the factory down and roast us all in the fire like – like rabbits.

TATIANA (*annoyed*). So you're drunk already.

YAKOV. By this time of day I'm always drunk already. I've just seen Kleopatra – she really is a worthless bitch. Not because she has all those lovers, but because there's a vicious old dog squatting where her heart should be.

PAULINA (*getting up*). Oh God. . . . Everything was going so smoothly, and then suddenly . . . (*She walks up and down the garden.*)

YAKOV. A very small dog. With a mangy coat. A small *greedy* dog . . . sitting there, baring its teeth . . . It's full up, it's eaten everything in sight, but it still wants something more . . . doesn't know what, so it gets in a state . . .

TATIANA. Be quiet, Yakov. Look, here comes your brother.

YAKOV. I don't want my brother. Tanya, I quite understand that it's no longer possible to love me, but, still, I don't like it. Don't like it, and don't stop loving you.

TATIANA. Why don't you freshen yourself up?

ZAKHAR (*coming up to them*). Well, have they announced that the factory's closing down yet?

TATIANA. I don't know.

YAKOV. It hasn't been announced, but the workers know.

ZAKHAR. Why? Who told them?

YAKOV. I did. I went and told them.

PAULINA (*comes up to him*). Whatever for?

YAKOV (*shrugs*). I just did. They're interested. I tell them everything – when they'll listen. I think they're quite fond of me. They like to see that the boss's brother is a drunkard, it makes them feel that all men are equals.

ZAKHAR. Hm. You go to the factory quite a lot, Yakov, and of course I've no objection. But Mikhail Vassilich says that when you're chatting to the workers you sometimes criticize the way the factory's managed.

YAKOV. He's lying. I don't know a thing about management. Or mismanagement.

ZAKHAR. He also says that you sometimes take vodka with you.

YAKOV. More lies. I don't take it with me, I send out for it. And not sometimes. Always. Don't you understand that I'm of no interest to them without my vodka.

ZAKHAR. But, Yakov, surely you can see – I mean, as the boss's brother . . .

YAKOV. That's not my only failing.

ZAKHAR (*offended*). Well, I'll say no more. I'll say no more. There's an atmosphere of hostility growing up around me which I just don't understand.

PAULINA. It's true. You should have heard what Nadya was saying a moment ago.

POLOGGY *enters, running.*

POLOGGY. Sir . . . may I tell you . . . it's the director . . . he's just – just been . . . shot, er, killed.

ZAKHAR. What?

PAULINA. You – What did you say?

POLOGGY. Killed outright . . . fell down . . .

ZAKHAR. Who . . . who shot him?

POLOGGY. The workers.

PAULINA. Have they been arrested?

ZAKHAR. Is the doctor there?

POLOGGY. I don't know.

PAULINA. Yakov Ivanich, do go!

YAKOV (*gesturing helplessly*). Go where?

PAULINA. How did it happen?

POLOGGY. The director got . . . in a state of . . . some agitation . . . and his foot . . . hit the stomach . . . of one of the workers.

YAKOV. They're coming now.

Noise. MIKHAIL *is led in, supported on one side by* LEVSHIN, *a balding elderly worker, on the other by* NIKOLAI. *Various workers and clerks follow, and then a* POLICEMAN, KLEO-PATRA *and* NADYA.

MIKHAIL (*wearily*). Let me go. . . . Put me down . . .

NIKOLAI. Did you see who fired?

MIKHAIL. I'm tired. Oh, I'm so tired . . .

NIKOLAI (*insistent*). Do you know who fired?

MIKHAIL. It hurts. . . . A man with red hair. . . . Put me down . . .

They lay him on the lawn couch.

NIKOLAI (*to the* POLICEMAN). You hear? A red-haired man.

POLICEMAN. Yes, sir.

MIKHAIL. It's not important . . . now. . . . He had green eyes.

LEVSHIN. You should leave him rest now, sir.

NIKOLAI. Hold your tongue. Where's the doctor? The doctor? I want to know where the doctor is!

Everyone fusses around, whispering.

MIKHAIL. Don't shout . . . it hurts . . . do let me rest . . .

LEVSHIN. Ay, you rest there, Mikhail Vassilich, and don't you worry. Ah, human affairs, copeck affairs! We go down for a copeck, it's mother to us and death to us.

NIKOLAI. Officer! Get rid of everyone who isn't needed here.

POLICEMAN (*quietly*). Off you go, lads. There's nothing to see here.

ZAKHAR (*quietly*). Where's the doctor?

NIKOLAI. Misha! . . . Misha! . . . (*He bends over his brother; others join him.*) I think . . . he's gone. He has.

ZAKHAR. No, surely –

NIKOLAI (*slowly, quietly*). Yes. He's dead. Do you understand what that means, Zakhar Ivanich?

ZAKHAR. [But . . . couldn't you be mistaken?

NIKOLAI. No. And] it was you who put him in front of that bullet. You!

TATIANA. How cruel . . . and . . . pointless.

NIKOLAI (*bearing down on* ZAKHAR). Yes, you!

The DISTRICT POLICE INSPECTOR *enters, running.*

INSPECTOR. Where's Mr Bardin? Is he badly wounded?

LEVSHIN. Gone. Finished. He chivvied them here and he chivvied them there. And now, himself. There.

NIKOLAI (*to* INSPECTOR). He managed to say it was a man with red hair who shot him.

INSPECTOR. A redhead, eh?

NIKOLAI. Yes. You should act on that at once.

INSPECTOR (*to* POLICEMAN). I want all red-headed men at the factory rounded up at once.

POLICEMAN. Yes, sir.

INSPECTOR. And I mean all of them!

The POLICEMAN *exits.* KLEOPATRA *enters, running.*

KLEOPATRA. Where is he? Misha! What is it? Has he fainted? Nikolai Vassilich, is he in a faint?

NIKOLAI *turns away.*

He's not dead, is he? Is he?

LEVSHIN. He's quiet now. ... Wherever it was, he didn't get there.

NIKOLAI (*angrily, but quietly*). You. Get out. (*To the* POLICE INSPECTOR.) Get rid of him.

KLEOPATRA. The doctor ... why isn't the doctor ... ?

INSPECTOR (*to* LEVSHIN, *quietly*). Go on, clear off.

LEVSHIN (*quietly*). I'm going. No need to shove.

KLEOPATRA (*quietly*). Have they killed him?

PAULINA (*to* KLEOPATRA). My dear ...

KLEOPATRA (*quietly, angrily*). Get away from me! This is your doing – yours!

ZAKHAR (*in a crushed voice*). I can understand ... the shock ... but why ... why say such a thing?

PAULINA (*tearfully*). Oh, my dear, that's a terrible thing to say.

KLEOPATRA. Oh yes? Terrible, is it?

TATIANA (*to* PAULINA). You'd better go.

KLEOPATRA. You killed him. You, with your damned flabbiness.

NIKOLAI (*coldly*). That'll do, Kleopatra. Zakhar Ivanich can see for himself how guilty he is.

ZAKHAR. I don't understand ... what are you saying? How can you accuse me like that?

PAULINA. How horrible! My God, it's so hard and unfeeling!

KLEOPATRA (*exalted*). Unfeeling, you say? You, who set the workers against him, you who destroyed his authority! They were afraid of him, they trembled under his eye, and now – there! There! They've killed him, and it's you – you who's to blame! His blood is on you!

NIKOLAI. That's enough. There's no need to shout.

KLEOPATRA (*to* PAULINA). Oh yes, you're weeping, are you? Then weep my husband's blood off your hands!

POLICEMAN (*entering*). Sir ...

INSPECTOR. Quiet!

POLICEMAN (*whispers*). The red-headed men, sir – they're being rounded up now ...

The GENERAL *appears at the end of the garden, pushing* KON
before him and roaring with laughter.

NIKOLAI. Sh-sh-h, please!
KLEOPATRA. Well, murderers?

CURTAIN

Act Two

A moonlit night. Thick, heavy shadows on the ground. On the tables, untidily, are quantities of bread, cucumber, eggs, bottles of beer. Candles burning, with shades. AGRAFENA *is washing plates.* YAGODIN *is sitting on a chair, holding a stick, and smoking. To the left stand* TATIANA, NADYA *and* LEVSHIN. *Everyone talks in hushed voices, as if listening to something. A general mood of unhappy, anxious expectancy.*

LEVSHIN (*to* NADYA). Everything human is poisoned with copper on this earth, lass. That's why life can seem dreary, even to your young soul. The copper copeck shackles us all together. Maybe you're free, still, maybe you've not found your place in the human chain, but the copeck chimes its message to every living soul – love me, as you love your own self. Nay, but that's nought to you.

YAGODIN (*to* AGRAFENA). Efimich is on to teaching the gentry now. He's a queer one.

AGRAFENA. Why shouldn't he? It's only the truth he's saying. The gentry can do with a bit of the truth for once.

NADYA. Is yours a hard life, Levshin?

LEVSHIN. Mine isn't too hard. I've got no children. I've got a woman – the wife, that is – but they all died, did the children.

NADYA. Aunt Tanya, why does everyone talk quietly when there's a dead person in the house?

TATIANA. I don't know.

LEVSHIN (*smiling*). That's our guilt, lass, before the dead one. We're all guilty, all round.

NADYA. But, Levshin, dead people haven't always been – killed. And whenever someone's dead, people talk quietly.

LEVSHIN. Ay, my dear, for we kill every one of 'em. Bullets for some, words for others, but it's us as kills 'em with our goings-on.

We drive folk from this world, into the earth, and we don't see it, we don't feel it. It's only when we chuck a body to his death like that, do we get a glimmering of our own guilt. [We'll feel a bit sorry for the dead one, a bit ashamed when we think on him. And then afeared in our souls. For we're all being driven the same road, all being readied for the grave.]

NADYA. Yes . . . it's frightening.

LEVSHIN. Nay, it's nothing. Today it's frightening, mebbe, tomorrow we'll not think on't. And folk'll be back at their pushing again. [One of 'em who gets pushed'll fall down, and they'll all be quiet for a moment – uncomfortable, like. Then they'll give a bit of a sigh, and be right back at it again.] Back at the old game. Poor ignorant folk, there's but the one road for all . . . But you've not felt your own guilt yet, lass, the dead don't worry you, you can talk loud before them.

TATIANA. What must we do to . . . live differently? Do you know?

LEVSHIN (*mysteriously*). Do away with the copeck! Bury it! Once that's gone, what's to quarrel about, what's to push at each other for?

TATIANA. Is that all?

LEVSHIN. It'll do for a start.

TATIANA. Shall we take a turn in the garden, Nadya?

NADYA (*thoughtfully*). If you like . . .

> *The two of them walk down towards the rear of the garden.*
> LEVSHIN *goes over to the table. Outside the tent appear the*
> GENERAL, KON *and* POLOGGY.

YAGODIN. So you'll even try sowing on stony ground, Efimich. You're an odd one.

LEVSHIN. Why?

YAGODIN. You're wasting your time. You think they'll ever understand? You might stir the soul of a worker, but never theirs. They need a different medicine.

LEVSHIN. The soul's another story, brother. At least these two are scratching the right itch.

AGRAFENA. Will you not have some more tea?

LEVSHIN. That I will.

They are silent. The hearty voice of the GENERAL *can be heard.* NADYA's *and* TATIANA's *white dresses are glimpsed among the trees.*

GENERAL. Or you can take a piece of string and stretch it across the road where it can't be seen. Someone comes along and suddenly – kerflop!

POLOGGY. It's a real pleasure to see a man fall down, Excellency!

YAGODIN. Hear that?

(GENERAL. Come on, I'll show you. Down to the fence, Kon!)

LEVSHIN. I heard.

KON. [There can be none of that tonight, with the dead in the house. You can't play jokes in front of dead people.

GENERAL. Don't try to teach me what I can do! When you die I shall dance the mazurka.]

TATIANA *and* NADYA *come up to the table.*

LEVSHIN. [The man's old.]

AGRAFENA (*going towards the house*). It's a terrible thing, him and his naughty ways.

TATIANA *sits down at the table.*

TATIANA. Tell me, Levshin. Are you a socialist?

LEVSHIN (*simply*). Me? No. Timofey and me are weavers, miss. We're weavers.

TATIANA. But you know some socialists? You've heard of them?

LEVSHIN. Ay, we've heard of them. As for knowing them, no, we don't know them. But we have heard of them.

TATIANA. Do you know Sintsov? In the office?

LEVSHIN. We do, that. We know all the clerks.

TATIANA. Have you spoken to him?

YAGODIN (*anxiously*). Why would we be speaking to him? Their place is up in the office, ours is down with the looms. When one of us goes up there, they give us the management's orders. That's all. That's our acquaintance.

NADYA. You seem to be scared of us, Levshin. Please don't be. We're very interested.

LEVSHIN. What's to be scared of? We've done no wrong. We were told to come here and keep guard, so we've come. There's some as are angry down there, saying, We'll burn down factory, burn down everything, leave nought but embers, but Timofey and me, we're against ugly deeds. Nothing must be burnt. [Why burn? Wasn't it us as built it all, us and our fathers, and our grandfathers? And then to go *burning* it?

TATIANA. You're not thinking there's anything harmful behind our questions?

YAGODIN. Why? We mean no harm to anyone.]

LEVSHIN. The way we look at it, what our hands have made together, is sacred. Men's labour must be valued justly, that's what. Burning don't help. But then, folk live in darkness. They like a fire. And they're angry now. The departed was a touch strict with us – may he not be remembered for it!

NADYA. What about my uncle? Is he better?

YAGODIN. Zakhar Ivanich?

NADYA. Yes. Is he any kinder? Or does he treat you badly too?

LEVSHIN. We don't say that.

YAGODIN (*grimly*). Strict or kind, they're all the same to us.

LEVSHIN (*explains gently*). The strict one's a boss, and the kind one's a boss. A disease don't pick and choose.

YAGODIN [(*bored*). Mind you, Zakhar Ivanich has a good heart . . .

NADYA. You mean, he's better than Skrobotov, then?

YAGODIN (*quietly*). The managing director is dead now.

LEVSHIN. Your uncle's a fine man, miss. But it isn't us as'll benefit from his beauty.]

TATIANA (*irritated*). Come on, Nadya. They don't want to understand us, you can see that.

NADYA (*quietly*). Yes.

They walk off silently. LEVSHIN *glances after them, then at*
YAGODIN. *Both smile.*

YAGODIN. How they do pluck at your soul!

LEVSHIN. It's all 'very interesting', for them.

YAGODIN. Or else they thought we'd maybe let something drop
. . . ?

LEVSHIN. That young one, now, she's a good little lass. A pity
she's rich!

YAGODIN. We'll have to tell Sintsov. Tell him the lady was
pumping us.

LEVSHIN. We'll do that.

YAGODIN. How about it, then? They'll have to give in, now.

LEVSHIN. Now he's not there, ay. What can they do?

YAGODIN (*yawning*). Ye-e-e-es. Ah, but I'm sleepy.

LEVSHIN. Bear up, brother. The General's coming.

The GENERAL *walks up towards the table. Beside him is*
POLOGGY, *walking respectfully, and behind him,* KON.
POLOGGY *suddenly seizes the* GENERAL'*s arm.*

GENERAL. What? What?

POLOGGY. A hole, Excellency, a hole!

GENERAL. Ah. Hm. What's all this? This – mess on the table?
Been eating here, have you?

YAGODIN. Yes, sir. And the young ladies.

GENERAL. That's it, then. So you're on guard duty, eh?

YAGODIN. Yes, sir. Keeping watch.

GENERAL. Good men. I'll speak to the Governor about you. How
many of you here?

LEVSHIN. Two.

GENERAL. Idiot! I can count up to two! I mean, how many
altogether?

YAGODIN. About thirty.

GENERAL. You armed?

LEVSHIN (*to* YAGODIN). Timofey, where's that pistol you had?

YAGODIN (*points to table*). There.

GENERAL. Dammit, man, don't pick it up by the muzzle! Here, why is it dripping wet?

YAGODIN. They must have put too much oil on it . . .

GENERAL. That's milk, not oil! What are you doing, soaking the thing in milk? What a ragbag you are! Wipe it, Kon. And teach these idiots how to hold a gun. (*To* LEVSHIN.) You, have you got a revolver?

LEVSHIN *indicates his breast pocket.*

LEVSHIN. Here.

GENERAL. And if these – these rioters come. . . . Will you shoot?

LEVSHIN. They won't come, sir. It's just that they lost their tempers. It's done with now.

GENERAL. [But if they do come?

LEVSHIN. They took it badly, the closing of the factory. Some of them have children.]

GENERAL. What's this song and dance you're giving me? I'm asking you, will you shoot?

LEVSHIN. Well, sir, we're prepared to shoot. Why wouldn't we be? But we don't know how. If it was shotguns, now . . .

GENERAL. Kon! Go and teach them. Take them down to the river.

KON (*sullenly*). Allow me to report, Excellency, that it's the middle of the night. It'll cause a lot of excitement if we start shooting now, people will come and want to know what's happening. But it's all one to me, of course. Anything you say.

GENERAL. See to it tomorrow.

LEVSHIN. It'll be all quiet by tomorrow. They'll open the factory . . .

GENERAL. Who will?

LEVSHIN. Zakhar Ivanich. He's having a talk with the men now.

GENERAL. The devil he is! If I had my way I'd shut it once for all. No more hooting in the small hours!

YAGODIN. We wouldn't mind sleeping a bit later, too.

GENERAL. You! I'd starve the lot of you! That'd teach you to riot!

LEVSHIN. We're not rioting, are we?

GENERAL. Silence! What d'you think you're doing, standing there? You should be patrolling the fence. If anyone tries to climb over, shoot. I'll answer for it.

LEVSHIN. Come on, Timofey. Don't forget your pistol.

As they leave, the GENERAL *shouts after them.*

GENERAL. Pistol! Greenhorns! Can't even call a weapon by its proper name!

POLOGGY. Excellency, allow me to take the liberty of informing you that the masses, by and large, are coarse and brutish. To take an example from my very own experience, sir, I happen to have a vegetable garden, and with my own two hands, sir . . .

GENERAL. Yes, yes. Admirable.

POLOGGY. Working of course in the free time at my disposal . . .

GENERAL. Yes, yes, everyone should work.

Enter TATIANA *and* NADYA.

TATIANA (*from a distance*). Why are you shouting?

GENERAL. Because I'm annoyed. (*To* POLOGGY.) Well?

POLOGGY. But almost every night the workers descend on my labours . . .

GENERAL. Steal your vegetables, eh?

POLOGGY. Precisely. I of course seek the protection of the law, the which is represented here by his honour the commissary of district police, a personage entirely indifferent to the animadversions of the general population . . .

TATIANA. Why ever do you [talk in such a silly sort of language?] (use such extraordinary words?)

POLOGGY (*confused*). I? Forgive me . . . but I studied for three years at the business college and I read the paper every day . . .

TATIANA (*smiling*). That explains it.

NADYA. You're funny, Pologgy.

POLOGGY. I'm delighted if I make a pleasant spectacle for you. A person should try to give pleasure . . .

GENERAL. Pleasure, eh? Don't you love fishing?

POLOGGY. I've never tried, Excellency.

TATIANA. Which? – fishing or loving?

POLOGGY (*embarrassed*). The former.

TATIANA. And the latter?

POLOGGY. I have tried the – the latter.

TATIANA. Are you married?

POLOGGY. It is my dearest wish. But as I earn only thirty roubles a month . . .

Enter KLEOPATRA *and* NIKOLAI, *walking rapidly.*

. . . I cannot venture upon such an undertaking.

NIKOLAI (*agitated*). It's beyond belief! Utter chaos!

KLEOPATRA. How dare he! How could he!

GENERAL. What's going on?

KLEOPATRA (*shouting*). Your nephew is . . . completely, totally gutless! He's agreed to all the demands of the ruffians – my husband's murderers!

NADYA (*quietly*). They're surely not all murderers?

KLEOPATRA. Making a mockery of his corpse, and of me! To open the factory before there's even been time to bury the man who was murdered because he closed it!

NADYA. But Uncle was afraid they'd burn everything down . . .

KLEOPATRA. Be quiet. You're only a child.

NIKOLAI. And that young fitter's speech – a clear call for socialism!

KLEOPATRA. Some young clerk's ordering everyone around, advising everyone . . . He even dared to suggest that the crime was provoked by the victim himself!

NIKOLAI (*making a note in a notebook*). Very suspicious, that character. He's too clever by half for a clerk.

TATIANA. Do you mean Sintsov?

NIKOLAI. I do indeed.

KLEOPATRA. I feel as if someone had spat in my face.

POLOGGY. Allow me to remark, Excellency, that when Mr
Sintsov reads the newspapers he makes numerous political
comments which are far from impartial . . .

TATIANA (*to* NIKOLAI). Does that interest you?

NIKOLAI (*defiantly*). Certainly! Did you think you'd embarrass
me?

TATIANA. I think we can do without Mr Pologgy's presence.

POLOGGY. Excuse me. I'll go, of course . . . (POLOGGY *exits
quickly, left.*)

KLEOPATRA. He's coming here. No, I won't . . . I can't see him . . .

NADYA. What's happening?

GENERAL. I'm too old for all this to-do. Killing. Rioting. Zakhar
should have foreseen all this when he invited me here for a
rest. [I shall tell him that it doesn't suit me. Yes. That's what
I'll do.]

> ZAKHAR *enters, excited but pleased. He sees* NIKOLAI *and
> stops in embarrassment, adjusts his spectacles.*

Listen, my dear chap . . . er . . . do you know what you've done?

ZAKHAR. Wait a minute, Uncle . . . Nikolai Vassilich . . .

NIKOLAI. Sir.

ZAKHAR. The workers were in such a state of excitement . . . I
was afraid they might destroy the whole factory . . . so I – I
agreed not to close down. I agreed to their demand about
Dichkov too, but I made it a condition that they hand over the
murderer. They're looking for him now.

NIKOLAI (*coldly*). They could save themselves the trouble. We
shall find him without their help.

ZAKHAR. I feel it's better if they themselves. . . . Yes. We've
decided to open the factory as from noon tomorrow.

NIKOLAI. Who is 'we'?

ZAKHAR. I, er . . .

NIKOLAI. Ah, yes. Thank you for the information. But it's clear to me that on my brother's death his vote passed to me and to his wife. If I'm not mistaken, you should have consulted us on this question, not gone off and made a decision independently.

ZAKHAR. But I invited you to come! I sent Sintsov to fetch you, and you refused!

NIKOLAI. Surely you can see that on the day of my brother's death I can't be expected to attend to business?

ZAKHAR. But you were there, in the factory!

NIKOLAI. I was there, yes. I listened to some of their speeches. What of it?

ZAKHAR. But don't you understand, something had to be done! Your brother, it turns out, sent a telegram to the town asking for troops. They'll be arriving by noon tomorrow.

GENERAL. Aha, troops! Now you're talking! Soldiers – that means real business.

NIKOLAI. A very wise precaution.

ZAKHAR. I don't know. When they see the soldiers the workers' mood is bound to deteriorate. God knows what might happen if the factory remained closed. I think I did the right thing. I think it will prevent a riot.

NIKOLAI. My conclusion is different. You should never have given in to those ... creatures. If only out of respect for the memory of my dead brother.

ZAKHAR. Oh, God. ... But there was the possibility of another tragedy!

NIKOLAI. That's nothing to do with me.

ZAKHAR. Possibly. But what about me? I'm the one who has to live with the workers. And if it came to bloodshed ... and anyway, they might destroy the entire factory.

NIKOLAI. That I don't believe.

GENERAL. Nor do I.

ZAKHAR (*crushed*). So you condemn my action?

NIKOLAI. Yes, I do.

ZAKHAR (*candidly*). Why is there all this hostility? I want only one thing – to avoid the disaster which could so easily happen.

I don't want any bloodshed! Surely it's not impossible to find some peaceful, reasonable way of living? But you look at me with hate in your eyes, the workers with distrust . . . And all I want is what's right, what's right and good.

GENERAL. Good, good – what's that? Only a word – not even that – a bunch of letters! G for George, O for Oboe, D for Dog. . . . Got nothing to do with getting on with the job. Eh? How's that?

NADYA (*with tears*). Stop it, grandfather! Uncle, don't worry, he doesn't understand. Oh, but Nikolai Vassilich, how is it that *you* can't understand? You're so clever, why can't you trust my uncle?

NIKOLAI. Excuse me, Zakhar Ivanich, I shall go. I cannot – I am not in the habit of discussing business with children. (*Exits.*)

ZAKHAR. You see how it is, Nadya . . .

NADYA (*taking his hand*). It doesn't matter, it doesn't matter. The important thing is for the workers to be satisfied. There are so many of them, and so few of us, and . . .

ZAKHAR. Just a minute, Nadya. I have to tell you that I'm very displeased with you. Very.

GENERAL. So am I.

ZAKHAR. You sympathize with the workers. It's only natural at your age. But you mustn't lose all sense of proportion, my dear. Look how you brought Grekov to the table this morning . . . I know him, he's a very bright lad, but all the same you shouldn't have made a scene with your aunt on his account.

GENERAL. [That's the stuff to give her!

NADYA. But you don't even know what happened!

ZAKHAR. Believe me, I know more than you do.] Our people are coarse and uncultivated. If you offer them a finger they'll grab your whole arm.

TATIANA (*quietly*). As a drowning man grabs a straw.

ZAKHAR. There's a lot of sheer animal greed in them. They need to be trained, not spoilt. Yes, trained. Kindly give that some thought.

GENERAL. Now I've got something to say. You talk to me Devil
only knows how, miss. Let me remind you that it'll take you
forty years to reach my age. Then, perhaps, I'll allow you to
talk to me as an equal, not before. D'you understand? (*Shouts.*)
Kon!

KON (*from behind some trees*). Here, sir.

GENERAL. Where's that – what'sisname – Frog?

KON. What frog, sir?

GENERAL. You know, that – what'sisname – Cloggy . . . Floggy...
Troggy . . .

KON. Pologgy? I don't know, sir.

GENERAL. Find him.

> *He goes into the tent.* ZAKHAR, *head bowed, walks back and
> forth, cleaning his spectacles with a handkerchief.* NADYA *sits
> thoughtfully on a chair.* TATIANA *stands watching them.* KON
> *exits.*

ZAKHAR. They say, we don't know who did it, but we'll find out.
Of course they know! I think. . . . (*He glances round, lowers his
voice.*) I think they're all in it. It's a plot. To be honest, he did
madden them, he used to make fools of them. Mock them. It
was almost an illness with him, his love of power. And they –
you know, they're frightening, their simplicity is frightening!
They've killed a man, and yet they can look at you with such
clear eyes – as if they didn't realize a crime had been committed
at all. That terrifying simplicity!

NADYA. Why don't you sit down?

ZAKHAR. [Why did he send for troops? Why? They found out
about it, of course. They find out everything. It may even have
helped to kill him. Of course I had to open the factory –
otherwise my relations with them would have been ruined for
ages.] At a moment like this they have to be treated with more
consideration, more leniency, not less. Who knows how it will
end? We must be ready for anything. Yes. In times like these a

wise man sees that he has friends among the people. . . . (*Enter* LEVSHIN *backstage.*) Who's that?

LEVSHIN. It's us. We're keeping guard.

ZAKHAR. Well, Efimich, now that a man's been killed you're all quiet and humble, eh?

LEVSHIN. We're always that way, Zakhar Ivanich. Always humble.

ZAKHAR (*reproachfully*). Yes. You kill humbly, too, don't you? Incidentally, Levshin, what's all this you've been preaching? All these wild ideas – we must do away with money, and bosses, and all that? You'd better drop that, my friend. You won't do yourself any good with that sort of talk.

> TATIANA *and* NADIA *go off to the right, where the voices of* SINTSOV *and* YAKOV *can be heard.* YAGODIN *appears from behind the trees.*

LEVSHIN (*calmly*). Now what kind of talk would that be? I've been living a good while, thinking a good while, and, well, I have things to say.

ZAKHAR. Not all bosses are brutes – you must know that. You can see I'm not a vicious man, I'm always ready to help you. All I want is what's best . . .

LEVSHIN (*sighs*). Who wants the worst for himself?

ZAKHAR. Can't you understand, it's *you*, I want the best for *you*!

LEVSHIN. We do understand.

ZAKHAR (*looking at him*). No. No, you're wrong. You don't understand. You're strange people. Beasts one moment, children the next.

> ZAKHAR *walks off.* LEVSHIN *leans on his stick and gazes after him.*

YAGODIN. Preaching again?

LEVSHIN. He's a Chinaman, that one, a real Chinaman. What's he trying to say? He understands nobody but himself.

YAGODIN. He wants what's best. He told you.

LEVSHIN. That's right.

YAGODIN. Let's be off. Here they all come.

> LEVSHIN *and* YAGODIN *retreat as, back right,* TATIANA, YAKOV, NADYA *and* SINTSOV *appear.*

NADYA. We're all walking round and round. It's like a dream.

TATIANA. Would you like something to eat, Matvey Nikolaich?

SINTSOV. What I'd really like is a glass of tea. I've talked so much today my throat's sore.

NADYA. Aren't you afraid of anything?

SINTSOV (*sitting down*). Me? No, nothing.

NADYA. Well I am. Everything's suddenly got muddled, so I can't tell any more which are the good people and which are the bad.

SINTSOV (*smiling*). It'll unmuddle itself. The thing is not to be afraid to think. Think without fear, right through to the end. Anyway, there's nothing to be afraid of.

TATIANA. Do you suppose they've calmed down?

SINTSOV. Yes. Workers so seldom win, even a little victory gives them great satisfaction.

NADYA. Do you love them?

SINTSOV. That's not quite the word. I've been living with them a long time – I know them. I know their strength. I believe in their good sense.

TATIANA. And that the future belongs to them?

SINTSOV. That too.

NADYA. The future. I can't grasp that idea – 'the future'.

TATIANA [(*with a laugh*). They're a cagey lot, these proletarians of yours. Nadya and I tried to talk to them, but we got nowhere.

NADYA. It was horrid. The old man spoke as if we were some sort of – villains – spies, or something. There's another man, Grekov, he looks at people in a different way. But old Levshin keeps on smiling as if he pitied us – as if we were sick!]

TATIANA. Do stop drinking, Yakov. It's quite awful to look at you.

YAKOV. What else can I do? That's what I ask everyone.

SINTSOV. Surely you can find something?

YAKOV. Don't want to. I feel a revulsion, an unconquerable revulsion, for business and everything to do with it. You see, I belong to the third category.

SINTSOV. The what?

YAKOV. The third category. People fall into three categories. Some spend their whole lives working themselves to death, others sit back and rake in the profits, and the rest – the third category – won't work because it's stupid and pointless, can't rake in the profits because it's stupid and embarrassing. So you see, I belong to the third lot. It includes all the idlers, monks, spongers and other parasites in this world.

NADYA. Why do you say these tedious things, Uncle? You're not really like that at all. You're just kind and gentle . . .

YAKOV. In other words, a good-for-nothing. I understood that when I was still at school. People drop into their own category at an early age

TATIANA. Nadya's right, Yakov. It's tedious.

YAKOV. I agree. Matvey Nikolaich, what do you think – does life have a face?

SINTSOV. Possibly.

YAKOV. It has. And it's always young. Not so long ago life used to look at me with indifference. But now it looks at me sternly and asks . . . asks, Who are you? What are you? Where are you going?

He is scared by something, wants to smile, but his lips tremble, he can't control them, his face is distorted by a pathetic, terrible grimace.

TATIANA. Stop it, Yakov, please! Look, here comes the prosecutor. I don't want you to talk in front of him.

YAKOV. All right.

NADYA [(*softly*). Everyone's so sad. All waiting for something to happen, and scared of it. Why won't they let me make friends with the workers? It's stupid.]

NIKOLAI (*coming up*). May I have a glass of tea?

TATIANA. Of course.

> *For a few moments they all sit in silence.* NIKOLAI *stands, holding his tea.*

NADYA. I wish I could understand why the workers don't trust Uncle Zakhar, and why . . .

NIKOLAI (*grimly*). They only trust people who exhort them with stuff like, Workers of the World, Unite! They trust that, all right.

NADYA (*quietly, hunching her shoulders*). When I hear those words – that challenge to the whole world . . . I feel we're all just in the way here – not needed on the earth.

NIKOLAI (*excited*). Exactly! That's just how any civilized person would feel! And before long there's going to be another cry echoing round the earth – Civilized People of the World, Unite! It's time to shout that, high time! The barbarian is coming, he's on his way, to trample underfoot the fruits of a thousand years of human endeavour. . . . He's on his way, driven by greed . . .

YAKOV. . . . and his soul is in his belly, in his hungry belly – and there's a thought to drive a man to drink. (*He pours more beer*.)

NIKOLAI. [The crowd is coming,] driven by greed . . . and 'organized' only by virtue of one desire – to grab and guzzle everything in sight!

TATIANA [(*thoughtfully*). The crowd . . . everywhere you go there are crowds . . . in theatres . . . churches . . . crowds of people. . . . But, I don't know, that's not quite right.

NIKOLAI. It is quite right.] What do these people contribute? Nothing but destruction! And please note that the destruction will be more appalling in this country than anywhere else.

TATIANA. It's always so odd to hear the workers spoken of as 'leading' something – it's not how I see them at all.

NIKOLAI. But you, Mr Sintsov – you, of course, don't agree with us?

SINTSOV (*calmly*). No.

NADYA (*quickly, quietly*). Aunt Tanya, remember how the old man talked about the 'copper copeck'? It's so simple.

NIKOLAI. And why do you not agree, Mr Sintsov?

SINTSOV. I have a different way of thinking.

NIKOLAI. A well-reasoned answer. But perhaps you'd deign to share your views with us?

SINTSOV. I'd rather not.

NIKOLAI. I'm extremely sorry. I shall console myself with the hope that next time we meet your attitude will have changed. Yakov Ivanich, may I ask you to be kind enough to see me to the house? My nerves are on edge . . .

YAKOV (*rises with difficulty*). Certainly, certainly . . .

YAKOV *and* NIKOLAI *go out.*

TATIANA. The prosecutor's a repulsive character. I hate agreeing with him.

NADYA (*standing up*). Why agree with him, then?

SINTSOV (*laughing*). Yes, Tatiana Pavlovna, why indeed?

TATIANA. I feel the same way myself.

NADYA (*walking about*). He was rude to me earlier. He didn't bother to apologize. (*Exits.*)

SINTSOV (*to* TATIANA). You may *think* as he does, but you don't *feel* the same way. You want to understand, but not him – he feels no need to.

TATIANA. For some reason I feel sorry for him. He's probably a very cruel man.

SINTSOV. He is. He's in charge of all the political cases in the town. The way he treats the prisoners is disgusting.

TATIANA. I ought to tell you – he wrote something in his note-book about you.

SINTSOV (*smiling*). Very likely. He has long talks with Pologgy . . . Indeed, he works very hard at it. Tatiana Pavlovna – I've a favour to ask of you.

TATIANA. I'd be delighted to do anything I can, believe me.

SINTSOV. Thank you. I expect the troops have been sent for . . . ?

TATIANA. They have.

SINTSOV. They were bound to be. That means a search. Could you help me to hide something?

TATIANA. Do you think your house will be searched?

SINTSOV. Bound to be.

TATIANA. Might they arrest you?

SINTSOV. I doubt it. Why would they? For making speeches? Zakhar Ivanich knows that all my speeches tell the workers to keep calm.

TATIANA. And there's nothing against you in your past?

SINTSOV. I don't have a past. Well? Will you help me? I wouldn't have bothered you, only I'm afraid all the people who might have hidden these things are likely to have their own places searched tomorrow. Passions were running so high today that a lot of people made public speeches. (*He laughs softly.*)

TATIANA (*embarrassed*). I'll be frank. My position in this household doesn't allow me to treat my room as my own . . .

SINTSOV. So you can't. Ah, well . . .

TATIANA. Don't be angry with me.

SINTSOV. Oh, I'm not. It's quite understandable.

TATIANA. Wait, though. I'll have a word with Nadya.

> TATIANA *goes off.* SINTSOV *drums on the table with his fingers, looks after her. Cautious footsteps are heard.*

SINTSOV (*softly*). Who's that?

GREKOV. Me. Are you alone?

SINTSOV. Yes. But there's people about. How are things now?

GREKOV (*with a smile*). Nasty. Really nasty. You know they promised to find out who fired the shot. They've got an investigation going now. Some of them are shouting, 'It was the socialists killed him!' – same old dirty song.

SINTSOV. Do you know who it was?

GREKOV. Yakimov.

SINTSOV. Never! Ha – I didn't expect that! He's so quiet and sensible. . . . How strange!

GREKOV. He's got a temper. Now he's set on owning up. Got a wife and child, and another on the way. I've just been talking to Levshin – he's got some fantasy about replacing Yakimov with someone less important.

SINTSOV. He's a queer old bird! But it is sad. And depressing. (*Pause.*) Look, Alyosha, you'll have to bury that stuff. There's nowhere to hide it.

GREKOV. I've found somewhere. The telegraphist – he'll take it . . . Matvey Nikolaich, you ought to get away from here.

SINTSOV. No. I'm not leaving.

GREKOV. You'll be arrested.

SINTSOV. So what? If I went away now it would make a poor impression on the men. No, it's better to . . .

GREKOV. That's true. But I'm sorry about it.

SINTSOV. Yakimov's the one to feel sorry for.

GREKOV. Yes. And there's nothing to be done. He wants to give himself up. Well – goodbye. Funny to see you guarding the bosses' property.

SINTSOV (*smiling*). What can you do? [My platoon all seem to have gone to sleep.

GREKOV. No they haven't. They're round and about, in little groups. Discussing things. It's a lovely night. Well, goodbye for now.]

SINTSOV. I'd like to come too, but I'd better hang on here . . . You're sure to be arrested too, you know.

GREKOV. We'll be inside together then. I'm off.

GREKOV *exits.*

SINTSOV. Goodbye. (TATIANA *enters.*) Don't worry, Tatiana Pavlovna. It's all been fixed up now. Goodbye.

TATIANA. I really feel very bad about it . . .

SINTSOV (*briskly*). Goodnight.

SINTSOV *exits.* TATIANA *walks softly up and down.* YAKOV *enters.*

YAKOV. Why don't you go to bed?

TATIANA. I don't want to. I think I shall go away from here.

YAKOV. Yes. As for me, there's nowhere I can go. I've already gone round every continent and every island.

TATIANA. This place is oppressive. Everything's crumbling, it makes my head spin in the strangest way. One has to tell lies, and I don't like doing that.

YAKOV. Hm. No, you don't like doing that . . . unfortunately for me . . . unfortunately . . .

TATIANA (*to herself*). But I've just told a lie – I said I'd talk to Nadya about hiding something – she'd have agreed, too. But I've no right to start her on that road . . . those people do sometimes take liberties . . .

YAKOV. What are you talking about?

TATIANA. What? Oh – Sintsov. It's all so strange. Not long ago life was so clear and simple, one could see what one wanted . . .

YAKOV (*softly*). Talented drunks, handsome idlers, and other such specialists in gaiety, have ceased to command attention, alas! As long as we stood aside from the dreary hustle and bustle, we were admired. But the hustle and bustle is getting more and more dramatic. 'Hey, you comedians, you clowns – get off the stage!' they're shouting. But the stage is *your* element, Tanya.

TATIANA. My element? I did once think that on the stage my feet were planted in solid ground . . . that I might grow tall. . . . (*Emphatically, with distress.*) But now it's all so painful – I feel uncomfortable up there in front of those people, with their cold eyes saying, Oh, we know all that, it's old, it's boring! I feel weak and defenceless in front of them, I can't capture them, I can't excite them . . . I long to tremble in front of them with fear, with joy, to speak words full of fire and passion and anger, words that cut like knives, that burn like torches . . . I want to throw armfuls of words, throw them bounteously, abundantly, terrifyingly . . . so that people are set alight by them and, shout aloud, and turn to flee from them. . . . And then I'll stop them. Toss them different words. Words beautiful as flowers. Words

full of hope, and joy, and love. And they'll all be weeping, and
I'll weep too . . . wonderful tears. They applaud. Smother me
with flowers. Bear me up on their shoulders. For a moment – I
hold sway over them all. . . . Life is there, in that one moment,
all of life, in a single moment.

YAKOV. Yes, I know. Living in moments is all we're capable of.

TATIANA. Everything that's best is always in a single moment.
How I long for people to be different – more responsive, less
careful – and for life to be different, not all hustle and bustle, a
life in which art is needed, always, by everybody, all the time!
So I could stop feeling . . . totally superfluous . . .

YAKOV *is staring into the darkness, his eyes open wide.*

What's wrong with you? Why do you drink so much? It's
killing you. You used to be so beautiful, you had an inner
beauty . . .

YAKOV. Stop it.

TATIANA. Do you realize how my heart aches?

YAKOV (*with horror*). However drunk I am, I understand it all . . .
that's the terrible part. My brain's so damned persistent, it goes
on working and working, every moment of the day. And always
I can see this face, this broad, unwashed face, staring at me
with enormous eyes which ask . . . 'Well?' Do you understand?
Just one word . . . 'Well?'

PAULINA (*running on*). Tanya, Tanya, you go, please . . . It's
Kleopatra, she's gone crazy, she's insulting everyone . . . You
might be able to calm her down. I can't.

TATIANA (*wearily*). Leave me out of your squabbles, can't you?
Get on and tear each other to pieces, and stop dashing about
trampling on other people!

PAULINA (*alarmed*). Tanya! What do you mean? What's wrong
with you?

TATIANA. I don't understand you. What is it you want, all of you,
what's eating you?

PAULINA. Do go and see her, Tanya. . . . Oh. Look. She's coming.

ZAKHAR (*off*). I'm asking you, will you please be quiet.

KLEOPATRA (*off*). It's you, you're the one to keep quiet!

PAULINA. She's going to come shouting out here, with all the men about. . . . Oh, this is awful . . . Tanya, please!

ZAKHAR *enters, with* KLEOPATRA *close behind him.*

ZAKHAR. For pity's sake – I shall go out of my mind!

KLEOPATRA. Don't try to run away from me. You're going to listen, I'll make you. . . . There you've been, currying favour with the workers, you just had to have their respect, didn't you? So you throw them a man's life as if you were throwing offal to a pack of ravenous dogs! You're humanitarians at other people's expense – on someone else's blood!

ZAKHAR. What's she talking about, for God's sake?

KLEOPATRA. The truth!

YAKOV (*to* TATIANA). I don't much care for this.

YAKOV *exits.*

PAULINA. Madam, we're decent, respectable people, and we will not allow ourselves to be shouted at by a woman with your reputation . . .

ZAKHAR (*alarmed*). Be quiet, Paulina, for God's sake!

KLEOPATRA. What's decent about you? Decent because you chatter about politics? And about the sufferings of the people? And about progress and humanitarianism? Is that it?

TATIANA. Kleopatra Petrovna, that's enough!

KLEOPATRA. I'm not talking to you! You don't belong here. It's none of your business. My husband was an honest man . . . straightforward and honest. He knew the people better than you ever will. But he didn't babble about them the way you do. And you, with your idiotic ideas, betrayed him. Killed him.

TATIANA (*to* PAULINA *and* ZAKHAR). Why don't you go?

KLEOPATRA. I'm going myself. You're loathsome to me . . . loathsome, all of you!

KLEOPATRA *exits.*

ZAKHAR. Did you ever see such a crazy female?

PAULINA (*crying*). We must give up the whole thing . . . we must go away! Insulting people like that . . . !

ZAKHAR. But why is she behaving like this? If she'd loved her husband, lived in peace with him . . . but she changes lovers twice a year. . . . And now, all this screaming . . .

PAULINA. We'll have to sell the factory!

ZAKHAR (*with distaste*). Give up? Sell? That's no way to talk, that's not it. No. We must think it out. Think the whole thing out. I've just been talking to Nikolai Vassilich – that female came rushing in and interrupted us.

PAULINA. He hates us, Nikolai Vassilich. He's full of malice.

ZAKHAR (*growing calmer*). He's embittered, and he's had a terrible shock. But he's a clever man. He's got no reason to hate us. And now, with Mikhail gone, there are so many practical considerations to bind us together. So many.

PAULINA. I don't trust him. I'm afraid of him. He'll cheat you.

ZAKHAR. Oh, Paulina, that's nonsense, you know. He has very sound judgement. He says that every hill commands a strictly limited horizon. Hm – yes. That's quite true, you know. And that if I try to see more than is physically possible from my hill, I'm bound to fall, and look ridiculous. And there's some truth in that, too. The fact is I've chosen a rather shaky position in my relationship with the workers, I have to admit that. This evening, when I was talking to them. . . . Oh, Paulina, they're so hostile, these people, they look at everything so – so suspiciously!

PAULINA. I told you. They're always enemies.

TATIANA *laughs quietly and walks away,* PAULINA *looks after her, and continues deliberately in a louder voice.*

They're all enemies, all of them full of envy, that's why they attack us!

ZAKHAR *paces quickly up and down.*

ZAKHAR. Well, yes, that's partly true, certainly. Nikolai Vassilich says it's not a class struggle but a race struggle – the white and the black. That's a crude way of putting it, certainly, it's stretching a point. . . . But . . . when you come to think of it . . . it's *us*, the people of culture, who created the sciences and the arts and so on and so forth. . . . Hm . . . equality . . . physiological equality . . . hm, well, maybe. . . . But first of all, become human, acquire some culture . . . then perhaps we can talk about equality.

PAULINA (*listening attentively*). I don't entirely understand what you're saying. You haven't spoken like that before.

ZAKHAR. It's all very sketchy, not thought out. But it's the way my ideas seem to be heading. There's something in it. One must understand oneself, that's the thing.

PAULINA (*taking his arm*). You're too gentle, my friend! That's why it's all so hard for you.

ZAKHAR. We know so little, so we often get a surprise. Sintsov, for instance – he surprised me. I'd got to like him for his simplicity, his clear logic. Now it turns out he's a socialist – that's where he gets his simplicity and his logic from!

PAULINA. Yes, he's very noticeable – such an unpleasant face! My dear, you ought to get some rest. Come along.

ZAKHAR (*following her*). And there's another worker. Grekov. Thinks the world of himself. Nikolai Vassilich and I were talking about his speech just now. . . . Only a boy, but the way he talked . . . such arrogance . . . !

They exit. Voices are heard singing in the distance. Then, approaching, hushed voices. YAGODIN, LEVSHIN *and* RYABTSOV, *a young boy, enter.* RYABTSOV *keeps shaking his head. He has a round, amiable face. The three of them stop under the trees.*

LEVSHIN (*softly, mysteriously*). It's all to do with the business of being a comrade, Pashok.

RYABTSOV. I know.

LEVSHIN. It's a common, human business, this, every man's business. Every good man is valuable now, brother. Folk are raising their heads, opening their minds, they're listening, reading, thinking. And any one who's understood something, is valuable.

YAGODIN. It's true, Pashok.

RYABTSOV. I know. Why all the fuss? I'll go.

LEVSHIN. Ay. But you mustn't do anything without knowing what it means. Without understanding. [You're young. This'll mean hard labour for you . . .

RYABTSOV. I'll run away.

YAGODIN. Mebbe it won't be hard labour. You're not of an age for hard labour, Pashok.

LEVSHIN. We'll think on't as hard labour. In this sort of business, it's best to expect worst. If a lad's not afraid of hard labour, you know his mind's made up.]

RYABTSOV. My mind is made up, Efimich.

YAGODIN. Don't hurry it. Think it over.

RYABTSOV. What's to think over? There's been a killing. Some-one has to pay for it.

LEVSHIN. That's it. Someone has to. We play fair – one of theirs has gone down, we'll pay with one of ours. For if one doesn't go, they'll get after several, they'll get after the best, and our cause will pay dearer, Pashok, than it'll pay with you.

RYABTSOV. [I'm not arguing, am I? I may be young, but I under-stand well enough. We've got to hold fast to one another, like a chain.

LEVSHIN (sighs). That's it. Without that, we're alone.

YAGODIN (smiling). We'll make a chain, surround them, pull tight, and that's it.]

RYABTSOV. Fine. I've been through all that. I'm single, so I should be the one to go. Only, it does make me sick to have to pay for *that* blood.

LEVSHIN. It's for our comrades, brother, not for the blood.

RYABTSOV. I mean, such rotten blood. He was a vicious man.

LEVSHIN. It's the vicious has to be killed. The good ones are no hindrance, they'll die of themselves.

RYABTSOV. [Is that all, then?

YAGODIN. That's all, Pashok. So you'll tell them tomorrow morning?

RYABTSOV. Why put it off? I'll tell them now.

LEVSHIN. No. Tomorrow's better. Night's a kind counsellor.

RYABTSOV. All right.] I'll go now then, shall I?

LEVSHIN. God be with you.

YAGODIN. Go on then, brother, Walk bold.

> RYABTSOV *goes off without hurrying.* YAGODIN *twirls a stick in his hand, staring at it intently.* LEVSHIN *gazes up at the sky.*

LEVSHIN (*quietly*). There's some fine young folk growing up now, Timofey.

YAGODIN. Good weather, good crops.

LEVSHIN. If it goes on like this, we'll make it yet.

YAGODIN (*sadly*). Pity for the lad.

LEVSHIN. Ay, pity it is. I feel it. He's a good dear soul, and there he's away to prison, and over a bad business at that. There's the one comfort for him, though – it's all done for his comrades.

YAGODIN. Ay. Pity, though.

LEVSHIN. Leave off, will you? [Ah, but why did Yakimov have to go and pull that trigger? Where does a killing get you? No-where at all. You kill one cur, the owner buys another, that's all about it.

YAGODIN (*sadly*). So many brothers going down.]

LEVSHIN [Come on, sentry. We're supposed to be guarding the boss's goods and chattels.] (*They start off.*) Ah, dear Lord!

YAGODIN. What?

LEVSHIN. It's a mess. Why can't we hurry up and get things straight!

CURTAIN

Act Three

*A large room in the Bardin's house.** *In the rear wall are four windows and a door, leading on to the verandah. Through the windows can be seen* SOLDIERS, POLICEMEN *and a* GROUP OF WORKERS, *among them* LEVSHIN *and* GREKOV. *The room does not look lived in: the furniture is sparse, old and of different styles; the wallpaper is peeling. A large table is placed along the right-hand wall.* KON *is angrily moving chairs about, placing them around the table.* AGRAFENA *is sweeping the floor. To the right and the left are large double doors.*

AGRAFENA. There's no call to be angry with me.
KON. I'm not angry. They can all go to hell. I'll be dead soon, thank God. My heart's on the blink already.
AGRAFENA. Everybody's going to be dead. It's nought to be proud about.
KON. It's enough. Everything's gone to rot. At sixty-five, dirty tricks are like nuts: I've not got the teeth for them. . . . They've picked up all those people: now they leave them to soak in the rain.

Enter, through the door on the left, BOBOYEDOV *and* NIKO-LAI.

BOBOYEDOV (*cheerfully*). Aha, so this is the courtroom! Beautiful! Well, then, here you are engaged in the execution of your official duties, eh?
NIKOLAI. Yes, yes. Kon, call the corporal.
BOBOYEDOV. We'll serve up our dish like this: in the middle, that – what's his name?
NIKOLAI. Sintsov.

---

* In the RSC production this set was a disused billiard room.

BOBOYEDOV. Sintsov. Very touching! And round Sintsov, the workers of the world, eh? That's it! Ah, it warms your heart! ... The owner, here, now, he's a nice man, really nice. Not so well thought of by our people, though. No. I know his sister-in-law, she played in Voronezh – a superb actress, I must say, superb.

> KVACH *comes in from the terrace.*

Well, Kvach?

KVACH. They've all been searched, sir.

BOBOYEDOV. They have? Well?

KVACH. Some cases positive, sir, some cases negative: evidence hidden. Wish to report, sir: District Police Inspector in a great hurry, sir, works carelessly.

BOBOYEDOV. Of course! They're always like that. Anything in the prisoners' rooms?

KVACH. Evidence hidden behind ikons belonging to prisoner Levshin, sir.

BOBOYEDOV. Well, take it all to my room.

KVACH. Yes, sir. [The young recruit, sir, recent transfer ...

BOBOYEDOV. What about him?

KVACH. Also careless in his work.

BOBOYEDOV. Oh, deal with him yourself, man! Go on!]

> *Exit* KVACH.

You know, he's quite a sharp one, that Kvach. Doesn't look up to much, in fact he looks a fool, but he's got a nose on him like a dog!

NIKOLAI. You ought to do something with that clerk ...

BOBOYEDOV. Oh, certainly, certainly. We'll squeeze him dry.

NIKOLAI. No, I mean Pologgy, not Sintsov. I feel we could use him.

BOBOYEDOV. Oh yes, that one, the one we were talking to. Yes, yes, we'll bring him into it.

NIKOLAI *goes over to the table and carefully lays out some papers.* KLEOPATRA *appears in the doorway, right.*

KLEOPATRA (*from the doorway*). Captain – would you care for some more tea?

BOBOYEDOV. Thank you, thank you, I'd love some! [It's beautiful here, really. A lovely place. By the way, I know Madam Lugovaya, you know! Yes indeed! Didn't she play in Voronezh?

KLEOPATRA. Possibly . . .] Well, how did your search go? Did you find anything?

BOBOYEDOV (*amiably*). Oh, we found everything, everything! We find things, all right, don't you worry. Even when there's nothing there, we find something.

KLEOPATRA. [I'm very glad. Very. My late husband took all these leaflets much too lightly, he said that paper never made a revolution.

BOBOYEDOV. Hm. Not quite correct, that, you know.

KLEOPATRA. . . . and he used to call those leaflets, 'instructions to fools issued by the central committee of lunatics.'

BOBOYEDOV (*laughing*). Oh yes, very nicely put, but not quite correct either, I'm afraid.]

KLEOPATRA. But now they've moved on . . . from words to violence.

BOBOYEDOV. Rest assured they'll be receiving a most severe penalty. Most severe.

KLEOPATRA. That's a great comfort to me. Your being here, Captain, made me feel easier at once. . . . More free, somehow.

BOBOYEDOV. It's our duty to keep society in good heart.

KLEOPATRA. And it's so refreshing to meet someone who's contented and healthy. They're such a rarity.

BOBOYEDOV. Oh, we in the Security Corps, you know, we're all hand-picked men!

KLEOPATRA. Shall we go to the dining-room?

BOBOYEDOV (*as they leave*). With pleasure. Tell me, where is Madam Lugovaya going to be playing this season . . . ?

KLEOPATRA (*dismissively*). I've really no idea.

> *They exit.*
> *After a moment,* TATIANA *and* NADYA *enter from the veran-dah.*

NADYA. Did you notice the look old Levshin gave us?

TATIANA. I noticed.

NADYA. It's all so beastly. And – shameful. Nikolai Vassilich – *why*? What have they been arrested *for*?

NIKOLAI (*coldly*). Don't worry, there are quite sufficient grounds for their arrest. And I must ask you not to use the verandah while there are . . . those . . .

NADYA. We won't, we won't.

TATIANA (*looking at* NIKOLAI). Has Sintsov been arrested too?

NIKOLAI. Mister Sintsov is under arrest, yes.

NADYA (*walking about*). Seventeen people! And over by the gate there's their wives, crying. . . . The soldiers push them about, and laugh at them – can't you tell them to behave decently?

NIKOLAI. They're nothing to do with me. Lieutenant Strepetov's in charge of them.

NADYA. I shall go and ask him myself.

> NADYA *exits through the door on the right.* TATIANA, *smiling, walks over to the table.*

TATIANA. Listen, you [sarcophagus] (tombstone) of the Law, as the General calls you . . .

NIKOLAI. The General is not a strikingly witty man. I wouldn't repeat his little jokes, if I were you.

TATIANA. [No, I got it wrong. The Law's tombstone, that's what he calls you. Does that annoy you?

NIKOLAI. I'm in no mood for jokes at the moment.]

TATIANA. Are you really such a serious man?

NIKOLAI. May I remind you that my brother was killed yesterday?

TATIANA. What's that to you?

NIKOLAI. I beg your pardon?

TATIANA. Come on, don't pretend. You don't have any real feelings about your brother. [Give me your arm – there – now let's walk . . . like this. No, you've no real feelings for anybody, no more than I have. Death – or, rather, the suddenness of death, has a bad effect on everybody, but I can assure you that not for a single moment did you feel for your brother with a true, human feeling . . . You just don't have it.] (You don't have any real feelings for anyone – no more than I have.)

NIKOLAI (strained). That's all very interesting. What do you want from me?

TATIANA. Haven't you noticed that you and I are kindred spirits? No? You should have done! I'm an actress, a cold person, wanting only one thing – a good role to play. You also want to play a good role, and like me you're a heartless, soulless creature. Tell me – wouldn't you like to be public prosecutor, instead of just assistant prosecutor?

NIKOLAI (softly). What I would like – is for you to stop this . . .

TATIANA (after a moment's silence, laughing). No. I'm hopeless diplomacy. I came to you with the intention . . . I was deter-mined to be nice to you, to be utterly enchanting. . . . But as soon as I saw you I started to be rude. You always make me want to – shower you with insults, whether you're walking, sitting, talking or – silently condemning people. But . . . I wanted to ask you . . .

NIKOLAI (smiling). I can guess.

TATIANA. Perhaps you can. But now it's no use, is that it?

NIKOLAI. Now, or earlier. It would make no difference. Mister Sintsov is very deeply compromised.

TATIANA. You rather enjoyed telling me that, didn't you?

NIKOLAI. I won't deny . . .

TATIANA (with a sigh). There you are – you see how alike we are?

I'm petty and vicious myself. Tell me – is Sintsov completely in your hands – I mean, actually in *yours*?

NIKOLAI. Of course.

TATIANA. And if I ask you to release him . . . ?

NIKOLAI. It will have no effect.

TATIANA. Even if I beg you?

NIKOLAI. It would make no difference. . . . I'm amazed at you.

TATIANA. Really? Why?

NIKOLAI. You're a beautiful woman – certainly an original one. Clearly you have a lot of character. [You've had every opportunity to arrange your life elegantly – sumptuously, even] and yet you go and get yourself involved with this nonentity. . . . Eccentricity is a disease. Any civilized person must be shocked by your behaviour. Nobody who admires women, who loves beauty, could forgive that kind of escapade.

TATIANA (*looking at him with interest*). So I'm condemned? Alas! Is Sintsov, too?

NIKOLAI. That gentleman will go to prison this evening.

TATIANA. Is that settled?

NIKOLAI. Yes.

TATIANA. Not even a concession in the name of gallantry? I can't believe it! If I wanted it – wanted it badly enough – you'd release Sintsov.

NIKOLAI (*thickly*). Try – try wanting it badly. Try.

TATIANA. I can't. I can't bring myself to. Still, tell me the truth – it wouldn't hurt just for once – if I did, would you release him?

NIKOLAI (*after a moment*). I don't know.

TATIANA. I do. (*She's silent for a moment; then sighs.*) What swine we are, the pair of us.

NIKOLAI. You know, there are some things that even a woman can't do with impunity.

TATIANA. Oh, rubbish! We're alone, nobody can hear us. Surely I'm entitled to say to you, and to myself, that we're both . . .

NIKOLAI. Please! I won't listen to any more!

TATIANA (*with calm insistence*). All the same, it seems you value those principles of yours less highly than a woman's kiss.

NIKOLAI. I've already told you I won't listen to you.

TATIANA. Go away then. I'm not keeping you, am I?

He walks out quickly. TATIANA *wraps her shawl about her, stands in the middle of the room and looks out on to the verandah.* [*Enter through door on right* NADYA *and the* LIEUTENANT.

LIEUTENANT. A soldier would never hurt a woman. Never. I give you my word on that. A woman to him is – something sacred!

NADYA. Come and see for yourself.

LIEUTENANT. It's quite impossible. The army is the last bastion of chivalry towards women . . .

They exit again quickly through the door on the left.]
Enter PAULINA, ZAKHAR *and* YAKOV

ZAKHAR. You see, Yakov . . .

PAULINA. But, think now, how else would you have handled it?

ZAKHAR. It's a question of facing facts . . . necessities.

TATIANA. What is?

YAKOV. They've got my head over a block.

PAULINA. All this extraordinary cruelty! Everyone's attacking us – even Yakov Ivanich, who's always so gentle. . . . We didn't send for the troops, did we? And certainly nobody invited the Security Corps – they always turn up of their own accord.

ZAKHAR. Blaming me for these arrests . . .

YAKOV. I'm not blaming . . .

ZAKHAR. You don't come straight out with it, but I can sense it.

YAKOV [(*to* TATIANA). There was I, just . . . sitting, and up he comes and says, 'Well, brother?' and I say, 'Foul, brother!' And that was all.

ZAKHAR. But you've got to understand that it's impossible, it just couldn't be allowed anywhere, to have the sort of socialist propaganda we've been getting here.

PAULINA. Take an interest in politics, certainly everyone should, but what's socialism got to do with that? That's what Zakhar says, and he's right.

YAKOV (*sullenly*). What kind of a socialist is old Levshin? He's just worked himself to a standstill, and now he's delirious with exhaustion.

ZAKHAR. They're all delirious!

PAULINA. You must have pity on us, my friends, we're absolutely worn out.

ZAKHAR. Do you think I enjoy having my house turned into a law court? But it was all Nikolai Vassilich's doing – how could I argue with him, after such a tragedy?]

KLEOPATRA (*entering quickly*). Have you heard? The murderer's been found, they're going to bring him in here.

YAKOV (*muttering*). Here we go . . .

TATIANA. Who is it?

KLEOPATRA. Some *boy*. I'm glad – it may be wrong of me from an humanitarian point of view, but I'm glad! And since he's only a boy, I'd have him whipped every day until the trial. (YAKOV, *grimacing, exits left*.) Where's Nikolai Vassilich? Have you seen him?

> *She goes towards the door, right,* [*as the* GENERAL *enters through it*]. *Laughter, and the tinkling of glasses, can be heard while the door is open.*

GENERAL [(*gloomily*). So there you are. All standing round like a bunch of wet hens.

ZAKHAR. It's a disagreeable situation, uncle.

GENERAL. What? All these security fellers? Yes. Can't trust 'em like real soldiers. That Captain's a thorough oaf. I'd like to play a trick or two on him – are they staying the night?

PAULINA. I don't suppose so – why?

GENERAL. Pity. We could have dumped a bucket of cold water over him when he goes to bed. I had them doing that with chicken-livered cadets in my academy days. Awfully funny, y'know, watching some naked feller leaping around and yelling, dripping wet!

KLEOPATRA (*from the doorway*). God knows what you're saying, General. Or why. That Captain's an excellent man, amazingly efficient. He rounded them all up almost as soon as he arrived. I think that deserves some appreciation.]

KLEOPATRA *exits*.

GENERAL. [Hm. In her book, any feller with long whiskers is 'an excellent man'. Everybody needs to know his own place, that's the point. Decency lies precisely in that. (*He goes towards the door on left.*) Each person keeping firmly in his own place. (*Shouts through door.*) Hey, Kon! It's you I'm after! There's a hole in the tent! (*Exits*)].

PAULINA (*quietly*). She really feels she's mistress here. Look how she behaves! Ill-bred, rude . . .

ZAKHAR. The sooner all this is over the better. How one longs for peace and quiet – a normal life!

NADYA (*running in*). Aunt Tanya, he's just a fool, that Lieutenant! I'm sure he beats the soldiers, too. He shouts, and makes fierce faces . . . Uncle, those wives *must* be allowed in to see the prisoners. Five of those men are married. Go on, please, tell that Captain, he seems to be in charge of everything.

ZAKHAR. [Look, Nadya . . .

NADYA. I'm looking, and you're not moving! Go on, please, go and tell him! They're *crying* out there! Oh, do *go*!]

ZAKHAR (*going out*). I don't think it'll do any good.

PAULINA. Nadya, you're always making trouble for everybody.

NADYA. It's you who's always making trouble.

PAULINA. We? What are you saying?

NADYA (*excited*). All of us – you, and me, and Uncle Zakhar – we make trouble for everybody. We don't *do* anything, but it's *because* of us . . . the soldiers . . . the police . . . the Security people . . . everything! And these arrests, too . . . and the women crying. . . . It's all because of *us*!

TATIANA. Nadya, come over here.

NADYA (*going up to* TATIANA). Well, here I am. What is it?

TATIANA. Sit by me and calm down. You don't understand any of it. There isn't anything you can do.

NADYA. And there isn't anything you can say. I don't want to calm down. I don't want to.

PAULINA. Your poor mother was right about you – you have an impossible character.

NADYA. Yes, she was right. *And* she worked, *and* she ate her own bread. But you – what do you do? Whose bread do you eat?

PAULINA. There she goes again. Nadiezhda, will you kindly stop talking like that! How dare you shout at your elders!

NADYA. What sort of elders are you? Why do you say 'elders'? You're just old.

PAULINA. These are your ideas, really, Tanya. You should tell her she's just a silly little girl.

TATIANA. Did you hear? You're just a silly little girl.

NADYA. There you are. That's all you can say. You can't even defend yourselves. Extraordinary people – there's really no place for you, even here, somehow, in your own home. Un-necessary people!

PAULINA (*severely*). You don't know what you're saying.

NADYA. Your house is full of soldiers, secret police, little fools with whiskers, all throwing their weight about, rattling their sabres, clanking their spurs, drinking tea, bellowing with laughter . . . and arresting people, shouting at them, threatening them . . . making their women cry. . . . And look at you. What are you doing? You've been pushed off into a corner.

PAULINA. Can't you see you're talking nonsense? These people are here to protect us.

NADYA (*with distress*). Oh, Aunt Paulina! Soldiers can't protect anybody from stupidity! How could they!

PAULINA (*indignantly*). Wha-a-at?

NADYA (*stretching her arms towards her*). Oh, don't be angry, please! I mean, everybody!

PAULINA *walks out quickly.*

Now she's run away. She'll go and tell Uncle Zakhar that I'm a rude, obstinate girl . . . and he'll come and make a long speech . . . and all the flies will fall off the walls from boredom.

TATIANA. How are you going to live? That's what I can't see.

NADYA. Not like this – not for anything in the world! I don't know what I'm going to do, but it won't be anything like the things you do. I went past the verandah just now, with that stupid officer. Grekov was standing there, smoking. He looked at me – and his eyes were laughing! Yet he must know he's on his way to prison – Oh, don't you see, people like that who live as they want to aren't afraid of anything! They can afford to laugh! I'm ashamed to look at Levshin and Grekov – I don't know the others, but those two . . . I'll never forget them . . . . Here comes that fat fool with the whiskers. . . . Ooo-oo!

BOBOYEDOV (*entering*). Terrifying! Who are you trying to scare?

NADYA. It's me that's afraid of you. You will let the women through to see their husbands, won't you?

BOBOYEDOV. No, I won't. I'm wicked.

NADYA. Of course. You're in the Security Corps, aren't you? Why won't you?

BOBOYEDOV (*amiably*). It's not possible at the moment. But later on, when the men are being taken away, I'll give permission for them to say goodbye.

NADYA. But *why* is it impossible? It depends on you, doesn't it?

BOBOYEDOV. On me, yes. . . . That is, on the law.

NADYA. What's the law got to do with it? Let them through, please!

BOBOYEDOV. What do you mean, what's the law got to do with it! Are you another one who doesn't acknowledge the law? Tut tut tut!

NADYA. Don't talk to me like that! I'm not a child!

BOBOYEDOV. Are you sure? It's only children and revolutionaries who refuse to acknowledge the law!

NADYA. Well, then, I'm a revolutionary.

BOBOYEDOV. Dear me. Well in that case I'm afraid we'll have to send you to gaol. Arrest you, and straight off to gaol with you!

NADYA (*unhappily*). Oh, do stop joking! Let those poor women through!

BOBOYEDOV. I can't! The law!

NADYA. The law's stupid.

BOBOYEDOV (*seriously*). Hm . . . You mustn't say that, you know. If you're not a child, as you say, then you must know that the law is established by the authorities and that the state cannot exist without it.

NADYA (*heatedly*). Law, authority, state . . . [Oh, my God. But aren't they all supposed to be for the sake of *people*?

BOBOYEDOV. Hm, well, first and foremost, I think, for the sake of order.

NADYA. Well order's rotten too if it makes people cry. All your authorities and states . . . none of it's any good if people cry. The state –] what nonsense! What good is it to me? (*She goes towards the door.*) The state! You don't understand a thing, you just go on talking.

   NADYA *exits.* BOBOYEDOV *is rather at a loss.*

BOBOYEDOV (*to* TATIANA). Quite a character, the young lady! But she's heading in a dangerous direction. Her uncle, I believe, is a man of liberal views, isn't he?

TATIANA. You should know. I don't even know what a liberal is.

BOBOYEDOV. Of course you do! Everybody does! Lack of respect for authority – that's what liberalism is. But I wanted to tell you, Madame Lugovaya, I saw you in Voronezh! I did indeed! I did so appreciate your acting – so subtle, so extraordinarily subtle! Perhaps you noticed me. I always sat next to the vice-governor's seat. I was an adjutant at the time, in the administration.

TATIANA. I don't remember. Perhaps. There are Security officers in every town, aren't there?

BOBOYEDOV. Oh, indeed there are, absolutely, in every town. And let me say, it's we in the provincial administration who are the true connoisseurs of art. [Possibly a few of the merchant class as well. For instance – take a presentation to a favourite actor at his benefit performance, you'll always find the names of all the officers of the local Security Corps on the subscription list.] It is, you might say, quite a tradition with us. . . . Where will you be playing next season?

TATIANA. I haven't decided yet. But of course it will have to be in a town where there are true connoisseurs of art – that can't be avoided, can it?

BOBOYEDOV (*missing the point*). Oh, of course. They're in every town, absolutely. You know, people *are* becoming more cultured . . . little by little.

KVACH (*speaking from the verandah*). Sir! They're bringing him in now, sir. The man who fired. Where do we put him?

BOBOYEDOV. In here. Bring them all in here. And call the assistant prosecutor. (*To* TATIANA.) Will you excuse me? [I must busy myself with a little work now.] (I must call the assistant prosecutor.)

TATIANA. [Will you be interrogating them?

BOBOYEDOV (*amiably*). Just a little, just scratching the surface, making their acquaintance, you know. Call it a quick roll-call!

TATIANA. May I listen?

BOBOYEDOV. Hm . . . Generally speaking it's not allowed – not in political cases. Ah, but this is a criminal case, isn't it? And we're not in a courthouse, are we? I would like to offer you some . . . ah . . . pleasure . . .

TATIANA. I'll be invisible. I'll watch from here.

BOBOYEDOV. Splendid! I'm delighted to be able to make even some small repayment for all the pleasure I've had from watching you on the stage . . . I just have to collect a few papers . . .]

BOBOYEDOV *exits. From the verandah* TWO ELDERLY WORKERS *come in, leading* RYABTSOV. KON *walks alongside, staring at his face. Behind them come* LEVSHIN, YAGODIN, GREKOV, *and a few other* WORKERS, *followed by* KVACH *and some* SECURITY POLICE.

RYABTSOV (*angrily*). Why've you tied my hands? Untie me!

LEVSHIN. Go on, brothers, untie him. No need to insult a person.

YAGODIN. He won't run away.

FIRST WORKER. That's the way it's done. It's the law.

RYABTSOV. I don't want it. Take it off!

SECOND WORKER (*to* KVACH). Can we, sir? He's a quiet lad. We can't understand . . . how he could have done it.

KVACH. All right. Untie him. It's not important.

KON (*suddenly*). There's no sense arresting that one. When the shooting was going on, he was out on the river. I saw him. So did the General. (*To* RYABTSOV.) Why don't you say something, you fool? Tell them it wasn't you! Why don't you? . . .

RYABTSOV (*firmly*). No, it was me.

LEVSHIN. He should know, soldier.

RYABTSOV. It was me.

KON (*shouting*). You're lying, you bastard! . . . (BOBOYEDOV *and* NIKOLAI *enter.*) You were out on the river in a boat when they did it. Singing songs, you were! Weren't you, eh?

RYABTSOV (*calmly*). That was after.

BOBOYEDOV. Which is the murderer? This one?

KVACH. Yes, sir.

KON. No he's not.

BOBOYEDOV. What's that? [Kvach, take the old man out. What's he doing here, anyway?

KVACH. In service with the general, sir.]

NIKOLAI (*looking intently at* RYABTSOV.) Allow me, Bogdan Denisich . . . [Leave him alone, Kvach!

KON. Keep your hands off me! I'm a soldier myself!

BOBOYEDOV. Wait, Kvach.]

NIKOLAI (*to* RYABSTOV). Was it you who killed my brother?

RYABTSOV. It was.

NIKOLAI. Why?

RYABTSOV. He gave us hell.

NIKOLAI. What's your name?

RYABTSOV. Pavel Ryabtsov.

NIKOLAI. I see. Now, Kon – what was it you were saying?

KON (*excited*). He didn't kill him! He was down on the river when Mr Skrobotov was shot. I'll take my oath on that! [Me and the General both saw him – the General even said, wouldn't it be good sport to upset his boat for him and make him take a bath. It's true!] What's this, then, boy? What are you up to?

NIKOLAI. Kon, what makes you so certain he was on the river at the actual moment of the murder?

KON. *Why, sir, the General and me came back to the house not five minutes after Mr Skrobotov had been shot and we'd just seen this boy sitting in his boat, singing. Anyway, you don't sing if you've just killed someone.

NIKOLAI (*to* RYABTSOV). Do you know that there are severe punishments laid down for anyone who makes false statements, or tries to shield a criminal? Did you know that?

RYABTSOV. That's naught to me.

NIKOLAI. All right. So you killed Mr Skrobotov?

RYABTSOV. Yes.

BOBOYEDOV. [You young animal!]

KON. He's lying.

LEVSHIN. Hey, soldier, it's none of your business, this.

NIKOLAI. What's that?

---

* In the 1906 text this speech of Kon's reads: 'It's two hours' walk from the factory to the place where he was . . .' For the 1933 production Gorky had altered this to: 'You couldn't get from the factory to the spot he was in even in an hour.' But even this reduction fails to make sense of the movements of characters in Act One, in which the General returns from the river, and Mikhail from the factory, only minutes after leaving the stage. In the RSC production it was imagined that the river was just at the bottom of the garden, and the factory gates not far beyond the trees that enclose the garden.

LEVSHIN. I say, the old soldier don't belong here, he's got no business interfering.

NIKOLAI. And do you have 'business interfering'? You're connected with this murder, are you?

LEVSHIN. (*laughing*). Me? I once killed a rabbit with a stick, mister, and it grieved my soul all summer.

NICOLAI. Well then, hold your tongue. (*to* RYABTSOV.) Where's the revolver you used?

RYABTSOV. I threw it in the river.

NIKOLAI. What was it like? Describe it to me.

RYABTSOV (*at a loss*). What was it like? Why, what they're like, you know, an iron thing . . .

KON (*joyfully*). Ah, backside of a bitch, he's never even seen a revolver!

NIKOLAI. What size was it? (*He measures about fourteen inches with his hands.*) This big? Well?

RYABTSOV. Yes. Well – a bit smaller, p'raps.

NIKOLAI. Bogdan Denisich, would you come here a moment?

> NIKOLAI *takes* BOBOYEDOV *to one side and talks in a low voice.*

There's something going on behind all this. That boy must be given some tougher treatment. Let's leave him for the moment.

BOBOYEDOV. But he's confessed! What more do you want?

NIKOLAI (*impressively*). But you and I suspect that this boy is not the real criminal but a substitute, do we not?

> *Through the door where* TATIANA *stands,* YAKOV *enters, cautiously. He stares in silence, sometimes closing his eyes. Now and again his head drops forward, as if he is dozing, then he jerks it up again and glances round in alarm.*

BOBOYEDOV [(*uncomprehending*). Aha, I see, yes, yes. Fancy that!

NIKOLAI. It's a plot – a collective crime. I'm going to make him pay for this!

BOBOYEDOV. What a villain, eh?]

NIKOLAI. For the moment, have the Corporal take him away, keep him in complete isolation. Complete! [I must go out for a minute –] (I have some further enquiries to make –) Kon! Kindly come with me. Where's the General?

KON. Digging for worms.

NIKOLAI *and* KON *exit.*

BOBOYEDOV. Kvach! Take this one away. And keep a close watch on him, right? Not a soul to speak to him, understand?

KVACH. Very good, sir. Come on, son.

LEVSHIN (*affectionately*). Goodbye, Pashok. Goodbye, friend.

YAGODIN (*grimly*). Goodbye, Pavlukha.

RYABTSOV. Goodbye. Don't worry.

KVACH *leads* RYABTSOV *out.*

BOBOYEDOV (*to* LEVSHIN). Old man – do you know that one?

LEVSHIN. Know him? Course I know him! We work together, don't we?

BOBOYEDOV. What's your name?

LEVSHIN. Efim Efimovich Levshin.

BOBOYEDOV [(*aside to* TATIANA). You just watch this.] (*To* LEVSHIN.) Now, Levshin, you tell me the truth. You're a sensible old man, I'm sure, and you know you must only tell the truth to the authorities, eh?

LEVSHIN. Why lie?

BOBOYEDOV (*with delight*). Splendid. Well then, tell me honestly – what's hidden behind the ikons in your room? Tell me the truth, now.

LEVSHIN (*calmly*). There's nothing there.

BOBOYEDOV. Is that the truth?

LEVSHIN. Ay, it is so.

BOBOYEDOV. Ah, Levshin, you should be ashamed of yourself. [There you are, bald and grey, and lying like a little boy! Now the authorities not only know what you do, they know what you

think as well! This is a bad business, Levshin.] What's this I'm
holding?

LEVSHIN. Can't quite make out . . . my old eyes are going.

BOBOYEDOV. I'll tell you. These are books, books forbidden by
the government because they call on people to rise against the
Tsar. They were taken from behind your ikons. Well?

LEVSHIN (*calmly*). So.

BOBOYEDOV. Do you admit that they're yours?

LEVSHIN. Maybe they are. One book looks much like another.

BOBOYEDOV. Then how could you lie like that, an old man like
you?

LEVSHIN. I spoke naught but the truth. You asked me what was
behind my ikons, and you wouldn't be asking that if everything
hadn't been took out. So I knew there was nothing there so I
said there's nothing there. Why try to shame an old man? I've
not deserved that.

BOBOYEDOV (*at a loss*). So that's it. Well, let's have a bit less of
your talk now, It doesn't do to joke with me. Who gave you
these books?

LEVSHIN. You don't need to know that. That I'll not tell. I've
forgotten. Don't you worry yourself about it.

BOBOYEDOV. Aha. Yes. Right. Alexi Grekov? Which of you is
Grekov?

GREKOV. I am.

BOBOYEDOV. Were you the subject of an investigation, in
Smolensk, into a case of revolutionary propaganda among the
workers? Mm?

GREKOV. I was.

BOBOYEDOV. So young, and yet so gifted? A pleasure to make
your acquaintance! All right, take them all out on to the
verandah, it's getting stuffy in here. . . . Vyripaev, Yakov?
Aha . . . Svistov, Andrey . . . ?

He follows the SECURITY POLICE *and* WORKERS *out on to
the verandah, checking their names against the list in his hand.*

YAKOV (*softly*). I like those people.

TATIANA. Yes. But why are they so simple? Why do they speak so simply, look at things so simply . . . and suffer? Why? Do they have no passion in them, no heroism?

YAKOV. They have a calm belief in their own truth.

TATIANA. [They must *have* passion. They must *be* heroes. But in here – didn't you feel it? – they just despise everyone!

YAKOV. Old Levshin's a good man. His eyes have such a look of understanding it all – they touch everything, so sadly and gently. He seems to be saying. Why go through all this, why don't you just move aside?]

ZAKHAR (*from the doorway*). They're really quite amazingly stupid, these gentlemen of the law. They've set up their little courtroom here – and Nikolai Vassilich is going around like some kind of conquering hero.

YAKOV. Zakhar, all you object to is that this business is going on in front of your eyes.

ZAKHAR. Of course! They might have spared me the pleasure! [Nadya's worked herself into hysterics. . . . She's been thoroughly rude to Paulina and myself, called Kleopatra a shark, and now she's lying on the divan howling her head off. God knows what's going on . . .]

YAKOV. But, Zakhar, it's the *significance* of what's happening that seems more and more sickening to me.

ZAKHAR. Yes, I know what you mean. But what can one do? If one is attacked, one must defend oneself . . . [I simply can't find a place to put myself in this house, it's as if it had been stood on its roof. . . . It's damp today . . . and cold . . . all that rain! Autumn's come early.]

ZAKHAR *exits.*
Enter NIKOLAI *and* KLEOPATRA. *Both excited.*

NIKOLAI. I'm convinced now that [he was bribed.] (Ryabtsov is shielding someone.)

KLEOPATRA. They couldn't have thought that up for themselves.

(*Calls to the verandah.*) Captain Boboyedov! (*To* NIKOLAI.) The man to look for is the cleverest one.

NIKOLAI. [You think it was] Sintsov?

KLEOPATRA. Who else? (*Calling.*) Captain Boboyedov!

BOBOYEDOV (*from the verandah*). At your service, Madame.

> NIKOLAI *and* KLEOPATRA *join* BOBOYEDOV *at the verandah door.*

NIKOLAI. I'm convinced, now, that the boy must have been bribed ... (I think we should move Sintsov into town for intensive questioning. I'm sure the socialists are behind all this ...)

> *He talks quietly to* BOBOYEDOV.

BOBOYEDOV [(*in a low voice*). Oh? Mm ...

KLEOPATRA (*to* BOBOYEDOV). Do you understand?

BOBOYEDOV. Mm, yes ... the cunning devils, eh?]

> *Exit* NIKOLAI *and* BOBOYEDOV *talking excitedly.* KLEOPATRA *glances round, sees* TATIANA.

KLEOPATRA. Ah, you're here, are you?

TATIANA. Has something happened?

KLEOPATRA. I hardly think it matters to you. Have you heard about Sintsov?

> YAKOV *glances at* TATIANA, *exits quietly.*

TATIANA. I have.

KLEOPATRA (*challengingly*). Yes, he's been arrested! And for my part I'm glad to see all these weeds being pulled up. Are you?

TATIANA. I hardly think it matters to you.

KLEOPATRA (*gloating*). You liked Sintsov, didn't you?

> *She looks at* TATIANA, *and her face becomes more gentle.*

How strange you're looking ... your face seems ... quite ravaged. ... Why?

TATIANA. Probably the weather.

KLEOPATRA (*going up to* TATIANA). You know ... this may be stupid of me ... but I'm a very direct person ... I've lived through a lot, felt a lot of emotion – and a lot of bitterness! I know that only a woman can be a friend to another woman ...

TATIANA. Do you want to ask me something?

KLEOPATRA. Tell you something, not ask. I like you. You're so free, and always so well-dressed. And you handle men so well. I envy you – the way you talk, the way you walk. . . . But sometimes I don't like you at all – in fact, I hate you!

TATIANA. That's interesting. Why?

KLEOPATRA (*strangely*). Who are you?

TATIANA. What does that mean?

KLEOPATRA. I don't understand who you are. I like everybody to be well-defined, I like to know what a person's after. I think people who don't know exactly what they want are dangerous, not to be trusted.

TATIANA. What a terrible thing to say! Why should I have to hear your opinions?

KLEOPATRA (*heatedly, and with alarm*). People ought to live close to one another, as friends, so that we could all trust one another! Don't you see? They've started to kill us now, they want to plunder everything we've got! [didn't you notice what terrible faces those men had? – like criminals!] *They* know what they want – they know, all right. And they live like a family of friends, trusting each other ... I hate them, I'm afraid of them. And we – *we* live like enemies, believing in nothing, bound together by nothing, each for himself. ... Look at us! We depend on soldiers and police and – and Security officers! – to protect us. They depend only on themselves. And yet they're stronger than us.

TATIANA. I want to ask you a question, too. Were you happy with your husband?

KLEOPATRA. Why do you want to know that?

TATIANA. I just do. Curiosity.

KLEOPATRA (*after a pause*). No. He was always too busy. And too handsome ... You found him attractive, didn't you?

TATIANA. No.

KLEOPATRA. That's odd. It seemed to me all women found him attractive. There's not much joy in that for a wife.

PAULINA (*coming in*). Have you heard? That clerk, Sintsov, turns out to be a socialist! And Zakhar was always so open and frank with him – even wanted to make him assistant book-keeper! I know it's only a small thing, but it just shows how difficult life's becoming. Your sworn enemies are right beside you, and you can't recognize them.

TATIANA. Thank God I'm not rich.

PAULINA. Say that when you're old! (*Gently, to* KLEOPATRA.) Kleopatra Petrovna, they want you to try your frock on again. And the black crêpe has arrived ...

KLEOPATRA. All right, I'll go. My heart's beating unevenly. ... How I dislike being ill!

PAULINA. I can give you some drops for the palpitations. They do help.

KLEOPATRA (*leaving*). Thank you.

PAULINA. I'll come in a moment.

    KLEOPATRA *exits.*

One must be gentle with her – it calms her down. It's good that you had a talk with her. I do envy you, Tanya – you always manage to find a comfortable middle position ... I'll go and give her those drops.

    Left alone TATIANA *looks out on to the verandah, where the* PRISONERS *are waiting under guard.* YAKOV *appears through a door.*

YAKOV (*grinning*). And there was I behind the door, listening.

TATIANA (*absently*). Eavesdropping's supposed not to be nice.

YAKOV. It's a bad thing altogether, listening to what other people

are saying. They just seem pathetic ... and boring. Listen,
Tanya – I'm going.

TATIANA. Where to?

YAKOV (*shrugging*). I don't know. Anywhere. Goodbye. And
forgive me.

TATIANA (*gently*). Yes. Goodbye. Write ...

YAKOV. It's pretty nasty here.

TATIANA. When are you going?

YAKOV (*with a strange smile*). Today. Why don't you go away too?
Mm?

TATIANA. Yes, I will. Why are you smiling?

YAKOV. I just am. ... You know, we may never see each other
again.

TATIANA. Rubbish.

YAKOV. Anyway, I'm sorry. Goodbye.

> TATIANA *kisses him on the forehead. He laughs quietly, pushing
> her away.*

You kissed me as you'd kiss a corpse.

> YAKOV *goes out slowly.* TATIANA *looks after him, makes as if
> to follow, then with a slight gesture, stops.*
> *Enter* NADYA, *carrying an umbrella.*

NADYA. Come out to the garden with me. Aunt Tanya, please.
I've got such a headache. I've been crying and crying like a
fool. I know I'll start up again if I go out alone.

TATIANA. What is there to cry about, my dear? Nothing.

NADYA. It's all so annoying. I can't understand anything. Who's
right? Uncle Zakhar says he is ... but I'm not sure. *Is* he kind,
Uncle Zakhar? I felt sure he was, but now ... I don't know.
When he's talking to me, I feel that I'm the one who's spiteful
and stupid. ... But afterwards, when I think about him, and
ask myself questions about the whole situation ... I don't
understand a thing.

TATIANA (*sadly*). If you're going to ask yourself questions, you'll end up a revolutionary. And founder in that hurricane, my darling.

NADYA. One must *be* something – one simply must!

TATIANA laughs quietly.

Why are you laughing? One simply must. One can't live one's life gaping at everything and not understanding anything.

TATIANA. I laughed because everybody's been saying that today – everybody, all of a sudden. Why?

They start towards the garden. The GENERAL *and the* LIEUTEN-ANT *enter. The* LIEUTENANT *steps smartly aside to let them pass.*

GENERAL. Permanent mobilization has always been necessary in Russia, Lieutenant. It serves a dual purpose – (*To* NADYA *and* TATIANA.) Where are you off to, eh?

TATIANA. For a walk.

GENERAL. If you meet that clerk – what's his name? Lieutenant, what was the name of that clerk feller we were talking to earlier?

LIEUTENANT. Pol - er - Ploddy, General.

GENERAL. Tell him to plod along to see me. I'll be in the dining room, drinking tea with brandy and the lieutenant . . . ho-ho-ho! (NADYA *and* TATIANA *exit on to the verandah.*) Thank you, Lieutenant. You've got a good memory, that's excellent. Every officer must be able to remember the names and faces of every man in his company. A recruit's a sly animal – sly, lazy and stupid. His officer has to get right inside his soul and arrange everything there the way he wants it, so that the animal becomes human, open to reason, and devoted to duty. . .

Enter ZAKHAR, *preoccupied.*

ZAKHAR. You haven't seen Yakov, Uncle, have you?

GENERAL. No, I haven't seen Yakov. Is there some tea going?

ZAKHAR. Yes, yes.

Exit GENERAL *and* LIEUTENANT. KON *enters from the verandah, looking angry and dishevelled.*

Have you seen my brother, Kon?

KON (*severely*). No. I'm finished with telling people things. If I do see a man, I'm not telling a soul about it. I'm done with that. I've said too much in my time . . .

Enter PAULINA.

PAULINA. There's some peasants outside. They're asking if they can postpone paying the rent again.

ZAKHAR. Oh, really! What a time to choose!

PAULINA. They're complaining about the poor harvest. They say they've no money to pay you with.

ZAKHAR. They're always complaining. . . . You didn't meet Yakov, did you?

PAULINA. No. What shall I tell them?

ZAKHAR. The peasants? Tell them to go to the office . . . I'm not going to talk to them.

PAULINA. But there's nobody there. You know perfectly well that the whole place is in chaos today. It's nearly lunchtime, and that Captain's still asking for tea, the samovar hasn't been out of the dining room all morning . . . in fact, it's just like living in a madhouse.

ZAKHAR. You know, Yakov has suddenly decided to take himself off somewhere. These neurotics!

PAULINA. I'm sorry, Zakhar, but honestly it would be better if he left.

ZAKHAR. Yes, of course. He's maddening, always talking nonsense. . . . Just now he was going on at me about my revolver, wanted to go shooting rooks or something. . . . He got quite rude. In the end he just walked off with it. He's always drunk. . .

Enter SINTSOV *from the verandah, with* TWO SOLDIERS *and* KVACH. PAULINA *looks at* SINTSOV *in silence through her lorgnettes, then goes out.* ZAKHAR *adjusts his spectacles in embarrassment, then moves aside.*

[(*Reproachfully.*) Well, Mr Sintsov, this is very sad. I'm extremely sorry for you. Extremely.

SINTSOV (*smiling*). Don't bother yourself. It's not worth it.

ZAKHAR. Indeed it is! People should always sympathize with each other. Even if a man I've trusted hasn't justified that trust, if I see him in adversity it's my duty to sympathize with him. Certainly.] Well – goodbye, Mr Sintsov.

SINTSOV. Goodbye.

ZAKHAR. [You've no complaints you want to make to me?

SINTSOV. Absolutely none.

ZAKHAR (*embarrassed*). Splendid! Well – er – goodbye. Your salary of course will be forwarded to you – Oh yes, certainly . . .] (*He goes towards the door.*) But this is impossible! My house has turned into a police headquarters! (*Exits.*)

SINTSOV *smiles.* KVACH *has been staring at him intently all this time, particularly at his hands.* SINTSOV *notices, and for some seconds stares into* KVACH'S *face.* KVACH *laughs.*

SINTSOV. Well? [What is it?] (What's amusing you?)

KVACH (*joyfully*). Nothing! Nothing!

BOBOYEDOV (*coming in*). Mr Sintsov, you'll be going into town now . . .

KVACH (*joyfully*). Sir, this is not Mr Sintsov! It's something else entirely!

BOBOYEDOV. What? Explain yourself!

KVACH. I know him, sir! He was at the Bryansk works, and his name there was Maxim Markov. We arrested him there two years ago, sir. This gentleman's no clerk, sir, he's just a metal worker, and he's got no nail on his left thumb. I know. He must have escaped from somewhere, if he's living on false papers!

BOBOYEDOV (*pleasantly surprised*). Is this true, Mr Sintsov?

KVACH. It's all true, sir.

BOBOYEDOV. Why don't you say something, eh? Let's see your
hand. . . . Is there a nail on the thumb, Kvach?

KVACH. No, of course not!

BOBOYEDOV. What's your correct name, then?

SINTSOV (*calmly*). Whatever you like.

BOBOYEDOV. And so you're not Sintsov! Tut-tut-tut.

SINTSOV. Whoever I am, you're obliged to be civil to me.
Remember that, please.

BOBOYEDOV. Oho! I can see from the start we're dealing with a
serious character here! Kvach, [take him into town yourself –]
(you wait here –) and watch him like a hawk!

KVACH. Sir!

BOBOYEDOV (*cheerfully*). [Well, now, Mr Sintsov, or whatever
your name is, you're off to town. Kvach, you report to the chief,
tell him everything you know about this character, and ask for
the file on the earlier case to be sent for. . . . No, don't, I'll do
that myself. Wait here, Kvach . . .]

BOBOYEDOV *goes out quietly.*

KVACH (*amiably*). Well, we meet again.

SINTSOV (*smiling*). Are you pleased?

KVACH. Course I am. Meeting an old acquaintance . . .

SINTSOV (*with distaste*). It's time you gave up this business, you
know. An old dog like you, with grey hairs, still hunting people
down – don't you find it humiliating?

KVACH (*amiably*). Course not. I'm used to it. I been in the service
twenty-three years. And I'm not a dog, neither. My superiors
have a great respect for me. Oh yes. Promised me an order.
Cross of St Anne. How about that? I'll get it now, too.

SINTSOV. Because of me?

KVACH. Yes. Because of you. Where did you escape from, then?

SINTSOV. You'll find out.

KVACH. Oh, we will, don't worry! Remember that dark fellow at
Bryansk, with glasses? Savitsky? A teacher he was. Well, he

was recaptured too t'other day. Died in prison, though. Very
sick, he was. There's not many of you, is there?

SINTSOV (*thoughtfully*). There will be. Just wait.

KVACH. [Really? That's good. The more politicals there are, the
better for us.

SINTSOV. More ribbons, you mean?]

> In the doorway appear BOBOYEDOV, the GENERAL, the
> LIEUTENANT, KLEOPATRA and NIKOLAI.

NIKOLAI (*glancing at* SINTSOV). I had a feeling about him. (*He
leaves again.*)

GENERAL. A fine specimen!

KLEOPATRA. Now it's clear where it all started.

SINTSOV (*with irony*). Listen, Mister Captain of Security, aren't
you handling things rather stupidly?

BOBOYEDOV. Don't you try to teach me!

SINTSOV (*insistently*). Yes, I will teach you! [Put an end to this
ridiculous exhibition.]

GENERAL. Just listen to that!

BOBOYEDOV (*shouting*). Kvach! Take him away!

KVACH. Sir!

> KVACH *leads* SINTSOV *out.*

GENERAL. The man's a wild beast, eh? Did you hear that snarl,
eh?

KLEOPATRA. I'm convinced he's behind it all.

BOBOYEDOV. That's possible, very possible.

LIEUTENANT. He'll be tried, will he?

BOBOYEDOV (*with a laugh*). We eat them just as they come – we
don't need sauce on them!

GENERAL. [Jolly witty, eh? Like oysters, the villains! Schlop!!]

> *Enter* KON.

BOBOYEDOV. [Exactly. Now, sir, we'll soon sort the whales from
the minnows, and relieve you of the whole comedy.]

He goes towards the door as POLICE INSPECTOR* *appears on the verandah. He shouts through the door before disappearing through it.*

Nikolai Vassilyevich? [Where are you?] The Inspector's here.

All except KON *follow him through the door. The* POLICE INSPECTOR *comes on from the verandah.*

INSPECTOR (*to* KON). Will the interrogation be in here?
KON (*sullenly*). I don't know. I don't know anything.
INSPECTOR. Table, papers . . . must be here. (*He calls out to the verandah.*) All right, bring them all in here! (*To* KON.) The dead man made a mistake – he said it was a red-haired man who shot him, but in fact he turns out to have dark hair.
KON (*irritably*). Live men make mistakes, too.

The PRISONERS *are brought in again from the verandah.*

INSPECTOR. Let's have them here then, in a row. You – (*To* LEVSHIN.) – you stand at the end. Aren't you ashamed of yourself, you dirty old crook?
GREKOV. Do you have to be insulting?
LEVSHIN. Never mind, Alyosha. Leave him be.
INSPECTOR (*menacing*). I'll teach you to talk!
LEVSHIN. Leave him. That's his job – insulting people.

Enter BOBOYEDOV *and* NIKOLAI, *who seat themselves at the table. The* GENERAL *sits down in an armchair in the corner, with the* LIEUTENANT *behind him. In the doorway are* KLEO- PATRA *and* PAULINA, *with* TATIANA *and* NADYA *behind them. Over their shoulders* ZAKHAR *can be seen watching crossly.* POLOGGY *appears from somewhere at the side, bows*

---

* In the 1905 text a new character called the Police Commissary appeared at this point. In the 1933 text he had been combined with the Police Inspector from the end of Act One, an economy which this version also adopts.

to the men who are seated, then stops, looking lost, in the middle
of the room. The GENERAL *beckons to him, and he tiptoes over*
and stands beside the GENERAL'S *chair.* RYABTSOV *is brought*
in.

NIKOLAI. All right, then. We'll begin. Pavel Ryabtsov.

RYABTSOV. Well?

BOBOYEDOV. Not *well*, you fool! *Here, your honour!*

NIKOLAI. So you insist you were the one who killed Mr Skrobotov?

RYABTSOV (*irritably*). I said so, didn't I? Why ask again?

NIKOLAI. Do you know Alexi Grekov?

RYABTSOV. How do you mean?

NIKOLAI. That one. Standing next to you.

RYABTSOV. He works with us, yes.

NIKOLAI. In other words, you do know him?

RYABTSOV. I know all of them.

NIKOLAI. Naturally. But you've been in this Grekov's house?
Gone for walks with him? In fact, you know him well, you're
very close, you're close friends?

RYABTSOV. I go for walks with everybody. We're all friends.

NIKOLAI. Are you? I think you're lying. Mr Pologgy, tell us –
what's the relationship between Ryabtsov and Grekov?

POLOGGY. A relationship, sir, of very close friendship. The face
of the matter is, there are two groups here – the younger lot led
by Grekov, a young man of amazing impertinence in his
behaviour to those in superior positions, and the older group,
sir, headed by Efim Levshin, an old fellow, sir, fantastical in
his speech, sir, and foxy in his actions.

NADYA (*quietly*). Oh, the disgusting creature!

POLOGGY *glances round at her and looks at* NIKOLAI
enquiringly. NIKOLAI *also throws a glance in* NADYA'S
direction.

NIKOLAI. Well? Go on.

POLOGGY (*with a sigh*). These two groups, sir, are linked by Mr
  Sintsov, who's on good terms with everybody. This element,
  sir, is unlike an ordinary man with a normal mind. [He reads
  books. Various kinds of books. And has his own opinions –
  about *everything*.] In his residence, which is nearly opposite
  mine and consists of three separate rooms . . .

NIKOLAI. No need for all the detail.

POLOGGY. Excuse me, sir! Truth demands completeness of form.

NIKOLAI. Of course. But we don't have the time.

POLOGGY. His residence, sir, is frequented most frequently by
  a certain type of person, including a certain Grekov here
  present.

NIKOLAI. Is that true, Grekov?

GREKOV (*calmly*). Don't ask me any questions. I shan't answer
  them.

NIKOLAI. That won't help you.

NADYA (*loudly*). Good, good!

KLEOPATRA. What's this performance for?

ZAKHAR. Nadya, my dear . . .

BOBOYEDOV. Sh-sh-sh!

  There is a noise on the verandah.

NIKOLAI. I consider the presence of people who've no business
  here wholly undesirable.

GENERAL. Hm? Who has no business here?

BOBOYEDOV. Kvach, go and see what that noise is.

KVACH. There's a man trying to force his way in, Sir. Shoving at
  the door and cursing, sir.

NIKOLAI. What does he want? Who is he?

BOBOYEDOV. Ask him, Kvach.

POLOGGY. Do you wish me to continue, Excellency?

NADYA. Oh, the little swine!

NIKOLAI. No, wait. May I ask everybody with no business here
  to leave!

GENERAL. Excuse me, but how is one to understand that?

NADYA (*shouting boldly*). You're the ones with no business here, not me! You've no business anywhere! I'm in my own home, and I'm the one who can tell people to leave!

ZAKHAR (*agitated, to* NADYA). That's enough. You'd better go. At once. Go on, leave the room.

NADYA. I see. It's like that, is it? In other words, I'm the real outsider here, am I? All right, I'll go, but let me tell you . . .

PAULINA. Stop her, Zakhar! She'll say something appalling!

NIKOLAI (*to* BOBOYEDOV). Tell your men to close all the doors.

NADYA. You haven't a scrap of conscience between you! You're just heartless, pathetic, miserable creatures!

> KVACH *re-enters joyfully.*

KVACH. Sir! Here's another one shown up!

BOBOYEDOV. What?

KVACH. Another murderer's shown up, sir!
> *Enter* YAKIMOV, *a young red-haired man. He approaches the table.* NIKOLAI *stands up involuntarily.*

NIKOLAI. What do you want?

YAKIMOV. It was me killed the managing director.

NIKOLAI. You?

YAKIMOV. Me.

KLEOPATRA (*quietly*). Aha, you monster! So you've got a conscience, have you?

PAULINA. My God, what terrible people.

TATIANA (*calmly*). They'll win, you know.

YAKIMOV (*grimly*). Well, what next? Here I am. Eat me, then.

> *General confusion.* NIKOLAI *whispers something quickly to the* INSPECTOR. BOBOYEDOV *smiles in bewilderment. The* GROUP OF PRISONERS *is silent, standing motionless. In the doorway* NADYA *is looking at* YAKIMOV *and weeping.* PAULINA *and* ZAKHAR *whisper together. In the silence* TATIANA's *voice can be heard distinctly.*

TATIANA (*to* NADYA). Don't cry. These people are going to win.

NIKOLAI. Well, now, Mr Ryabtsov. Where does this leave you?

RYABTSOV (*at a loss*). Er – don't rightly know.

YAKIMOV. Quiet, Pasha. Say nothing.

LEVSHIN (*joyfully*). Ah, my good brothers!

NIKOLAI (*banging his fist on the table*). Be quiet, will you!

The SOLDIERS *start to close in on the* GROUP OF WORKERS.

YAKIMOV (*calmly*). No need to shout, mister. We're not shouting.

LEVSHIN (*to* YAKIMOV). *Well, go on then, lad. Tell 'em what really happened. Tell 'em how he was poking at you with his gun and . . .*

BOBOYEDOV. *Did you hear what the old liar . . .*

LEVSHIN. *Don't call me a liar, mister.*

BOBOYEDOV. *Throw him out, Corporal.*

LEVSHIN. *There's no throwing. You can't throw us all out. You'll never do that.*

KVACH *closes in on* LEVSHIN. *The* SOLDIERS *start pushing the growling* WORKERS *towards the doors, pulling bags over their heads to silence them.* LEVSHIN *struggles with* KVACH.

GREKOV (*quietly*). *No. You can't throw us all out.*

LEVSHIN. *There'll be no more of that. No more darkness. No more . . .**

NADYA (*suddenly, to* YAKIMOV). [Listen! you didn't kill him! It was them! They kill everyone, they kill off everything with their greed and their cowardice . . . (*To the others, as* YAKIMOV

---

* The lines in italics have been adapted from the rewritten ending in the 1933 text. In the RSC production the play ended when this line of Levshin's was cut off by his having a bag pulled over his head by Kvach, followed immediately by the shot, which froze the action. The shot itself is not mentioned in Gorky's stage directions, but it is perfectly well justified by the text.

is pushed back through the door.) It's you – you – you're the criminals!

LEVSHIN (*warmly*). Ay, lass. The killer's not the one who fires bullets, but the one who plants bitterness. True, my dear.]

General struggle and noise. Offstage, a shot. Silence.

CURTAIN